Boats in the Night

Knud Dyby's Involvement in the Rescue of the Danish Jews and Danish Resistance

Boats in the Night

Knud Dyby's Involvement in the Rescue of the Danish Jews and the Danish Resistance

Martha Loeffler

Foreword by Former U.S. Senator Paul Simon

Edited by John Mark Nielsen

Lur Publications
Danish Immigrant Archive

Dana College, Blair, Nebraska

Published by Lur Publications, Dana College, Blair, Nebraska, 68008.

First edition.

ISBN 0-930697-06-5

Cover designed by MicroSmart Printing & Graphics from a poster prepared by Claus Windelev for the Danish Home, Croton-on-Hudson, New York, commemorating the 50th anniversary of the rescue of Danish Jewry, June 6, 1993. Used by permission.

Logo designed by Elizabeth Solevad Nielsen
Designed by Thomas S. Nielsen, 2066 Colfax St., Blair, NE 68008
Digital & Scanner Services by Dr. John Greene, Greenbrae, CA
Printed by MicroSmart Printing & Graphics, 1740 Washington St., Blair, NE 68008

Printed in the United States of America

For Knud Dyby
and all other Righteous Gentiles,
known and unknown
and
in loving memory of
Dr. Erwin S. Loeffler

Lur Publications gratefully acknowledges
the following individuals and foundations
who have provided major support for the publication of
Boats in the Night:

Maurice Kanbar, San Francisco, California
Claus Lund, Belvedere, California
The Schultz Foundation, Albertslund, Denmark

and

Leitha K. and Willard A. Richardson
for their support of of the
Leitha K. and Willard A. Richardson Professorship
in the Liberal Arts at Dana College

Table of Contents

Illustrations

Foreword

Outside of the Jewish and Danish communities, few people know the story of heroism that took place during the Nazi occupation of Denmark, and this book should help reach a larger audience. We need to be reminded that people of courage must protect the rights of others.

As we read this book we identify with Knud Dyby and the other people of courage, particularly the people who operated the boats, often citizens with limited education but a strong sense of decency and compassion that caused them to risk their lives for strangers.

We are also repelled by the Nazis and the small group of Danes who opportunistically took up the Nazi cause. As Americans read this account there is a tendency to sense repugnancy at what the Nazis did, to feel a sense of moral superiority, and to whisper to ourselves that we would not do anything like that. I hope that is correct. But the history of humanity is scarred with wounds inflicted by people who should have known better; thankfully, most of those wounds have not been as serious as the Holocaust in the numbers of people affected.

The United States was one of the last nations to outlaw slavery. In February 1942, the President of the United States ordered 120,000 Japanese Americans to sell everything they owned in one to three days and put any possessions they wanted to save into one suitcase and they would be taken to camps. Not a one of the 120,000 had been charged with a crime or came under suspicion of sabotage. And almost no one in our nation voiced opposition to this gross abuse of human rights. Even the U.S. Supreme Court approved this action in the Korematsu decision, one of the worst in the history of that court.

So we should read this book with pleasure, with gratitude to those who gave us examples of courage--and we should learn that the defense of human rights is not made only by courts and high officials, but also by people with rough hands who fish, by bakers and carpenters, physicians and journalists, members of the clergy and police officials.

We should look in the mirror and ask whether we would have such courage.

- Paul Simon, Former United States Senator from Illinois

Out of a Clouded Memory

When I was bicycling around Copenhagen more than fifty years ago, I had no idea that in this great country of the United States of America I would be invited to speak about my experience in the fight for freedom against the Gestapo and German Wehrmacht and rescuing Jews and others during the occupation of Denmark between 1940-1945.

When the staff of the San Francisco Holocaust Oral History Project suggested to Martha Loeffler that a book about me would be interesting and could teach about altruism and righteousness, I had no idea how difficult it was going to be to recall events and activities from an old and disorganized brain.

In the "resistance" it wasn't wise to be caught with names or detailed information when there was a good chance of being painfully interrogated. The less you knew the better off you were. And because I never was what you could call a "detail-person," it was easy for me to erase and forget. That is why, in this story, there often is only a first name or a last name, as often I did not know anything else, even if I worked very closely with the person.

I tried to tell my story to Martha to the best of my ability. If I have told of names, dates or places incorrectly -- or even included in my own experience events that happened to friends -- it is not to misinform, but to let readers into the sphere of "Davids fighting Goliaths" -- ordinary everyday people sometimes being able to do extraordinary feats.

If the book seems to be an "ego-trip," please excuse. At countless presentations in schools, colleges, universities, museums, synagogues and churches, it was obvious that our story of rescue and resistance was appreciated and needed to be told in the English language.

Finally, when I talk about my small part in the rescue and resistance, I also like to tell about my personal philosophy of the "Three C's: Compassion, Conscience and Consideration." These three words have been the inspiration for everything I have done in my life. With *Boats in the Night,* we remember the courageous deeds of the past and hope to inspire those who read this book, young as well as old, of the need always to take individual responsibility, even under the most hazardous circumstances.

To quote Bishop Tutu: "Without memory, there is no healing. Without forgiveness, there is no future.

Knud Dyby
1999

What Would You Have Done?

It is 1940 and your country has been invaded and occupied by enemy forces. You are helpless and angry because your government has capitulated with barely a hint of resistance. New rules immediately are imposed governing almost every aspect of your life: food and fuel rationing, curfew hours and a gagged press. Already, terrible acts of random violence by the hated enemy have erupted. Anyone disobeying the new laws faces severe punishment.

You learn that the enemy is about to round up and deport the Jews from your country. You realize they will be sent to the notorious concentration camps you have heard about and you know that many, if not most, will probably die there. You are not Jewish. In fact, you know very few Jews, or maybe you know none at all. And there are threats of severe punishment for anyone caught helping the victims.

What would you have done? Would you have managed to ignore the rumors? Would you have tried to live quietly, taking as few chances as possible in order to assure your own safety and the safety of your family? Would you have been a silent bystander?

This is not an imaginary scenario. This is Denmark during World War II, from 1940 to 1945. *Boats in the Night* is the true story of how Knud Dyby and other Danes answered these questions.

Martha Loeffler

Knud Dyby as a police officer, 1941 to 1946.

1

On the Run

The wail of sirens, rising and falling, shattered the September air. The "luft alarm" (air alarm) as the Danes called it, was ear-piercing and frightening. Cars screeched to a halt and pedestrians fled into doorways and shelters. Copenhagen quickly became a ghost town as streets emptied and all the usual busy commotion of Denmark's capital came to an abrupt stop.

The date was September 19, 1944, and much of the world was engulfed in World War II. Adolf Hitler, Nazi dictator of Germany's Third Reich, was determined to secure his country's supremacy "for the next thousand years" and in the process his military forces had conquered most of the countries of western Europe. Denmark was one of those conquered countries, now occupied by the enemy.

Knud Dyby heard the alarm. A Danish policeman, he was off-duty at the time and had gone home for a few hours rest. In the normal course of events he would have rushed to work at the sound of the siren, as did every policeman, including most who were off-duty, but because he did not hear any planes overhead, nor did he hear the sound of anti-aircraft guns, he pedaled his bicycle at a leisurely pace while heading toward the police station.

An errant rifle shot almost blew his hat off and made him suddenly aware that this was not the usual alarm. Scrunching down and pedaling faster, he neared the police station and saw it surrounded by armed German soldiers forcing the officers into open trucks. Dyby did not know at the time, but in a bizarre, unprecedented move, the Nazis had decided to arrest the entire Danish police force! The police had not helped stop the rising sabotage or underground activities, and the Nazis suspected that some members of the force were participating in the resistance. The Germans knew that if it came to a show-down, the police would be in the first line of opposition.

German special police arrested 1900 policemen who were promptly deported and sent to concentration camps. About half of the force managed to escape capture and most of them joined the underground, even those who previously had not been actively involved in the resistance. Many found refuge in homes of sympathetic Danes.

Knud Dyby (pronounced Knooth Dye-bee) was one of those who escaped the Nazi net. When he saw the Germans arresting his fellow officers, he changed course and headed for an annex next to the station. Besides being a policeman he also worked as a local supervisor for the Civil Patrol and their office was in the annex. He hastily filled a big canvas sack with all kinds of material which could be used by the underground in its work, including forms for passports, birth certificates and identification cards.

Trying to appear nonchalant, Dyby donned a borrowed coat and brazenly walked outside with the sack, which was too big to carry on his bicycle. He hailed a taxi and as the cab took off the driver casually asked Dyby if he had his personal identification with him because a short distance ahead all cars were being stopped by the Germans. When Dyby replied that he had ". . . about 200 identification cards" in the sack, the driver quickly stopped. Together they put the sack on top of the taxi, neatly nestled next to a big bag of wood chips. Because of the shortage of gasoline the taxi driver was using wood chips as a source of fuel for his cab. Once again the cab took off, this time the driver carefully taking a side road to Dyby's place. "The false drivers' licenses and identification cards later came in very handy, but now I had to find a new place to live," says Dyby, recalling the incident.

2

Map of Denmark

The Wehrmacht crossing a bridge between two of the Danish islands.

2

Invasion & Occupation

Like all Danes, Dyby read the stories in the daily newspapers and listened to regular radio accounts that reported details about Hitler's aggressive military tactics in other parts of Europe. On September 1, 1939, Germany attacked Poland, followed immediately by Britain and France declaring war on Germany. It was the beginning of World War II.

In Denmark's local coffee shops and casual gatherings, rumors about the war circulated continuously. Although country after country was being engulfed by Hitler's military machine, the Danes assumed they would be safely on the sidelines, thanks to their 1939 declaration of neutrality and the non-aggression pact signed with Germany. Nevertheless, the Danes were uneasy and because of their geographic location, knew they were vulnerable. Denmark is composed of 482 islands and a peninsula, the Jutland Peninsula, which is surrounded by water except for the forty-two mile (sixty-eight kilometer) border it shares with Germany, its neighbor to the south.

In the spring of 1940, Knud Dyby was living and working in Copenhagen. He had become a member of the typographical union, but as one of its newest members he was "last one in, first one out" and when times were hard he was frequently forced to move from job to job. During one interval of enforced leisure, he went home for a brief visit with his parents in Randers, and it was during that visit he witnessed the invasion of his country.

Knud Dyby has total recall of that historic day:

The 9th of April, 1940, is a date no Dane will ever forget. I was sleeping in my old childhood room in my parents' home. Early in the morning I was awakened by the noise of hundreds of airplanes flying overhead. Like everyone else, I went outside and saw the sky almost blackened by German planes. Instead of dropping bombs they dropped leaflets. I grabbed one of the cheap paper leaflets and on it there was a message printed in faulty Danish language that told us that now we were a "protectorate" and the Germans wished to protect us and our coasts from an Allied invasion. They told us not to resist or there would be terrible consequences. That was the beginning.

On that fateful morning in April, at 4:15 a.m., while the country was sleeping, German army units crossed the Danish border into Jutland. At the same time, German paratroops landed at strategic points throughout the country.

Dyby's eyes glisten as he remembers:

I looked out at the German army flooding onto the railroad station right across from our home and spilling into the streets and the occupied school houses. I was angry and frustrated and saddened by what I was seeing. I did not think such a thing would happen. Also, it was during that day I learned of the death of my dear paternal grandmother, Lydia Dyring-Olsen, who had died in Randers at the very time the German planes flew overhead. Added to my own sorrow, the sight of the Germans was emotionally shocking and I felt as if they had stepped on my body and soul.

In an added display of strength, a German merchant ship, loaded with soldiers, docked in Copenhagen Harbor. Enemy soldiers quickly captured the Citadel, the Copenhagen headquarters of the Danish military General Staff. In order to avoid casualties to

German motorized troops enter a town in Jutland on April 9, 1940.

the population, King Christian X and the government agreed to capitulate rather than fight. In a short time the invasion was complete.

> *Now the radio and newspapers were telling us we should obey instructions and not resist the German forces and everything would be fine. It took a little while for this to 'sink in' and when it did, we had feelings of unbelievable suppressed anger. We loved being Danes and were proud of the knowledge that for centuries we had resisted the inroads of the Germans.*

An accord was reached with the Germans recognizing the authority of the Danish government and permitting the King to remain the titular head of the country. Danes were to continue to keep control over matters of domestic policy which included the right to maintain a token army and navy, a police force and their own judicial system. The Germans said they had no intention of interfering with the political independence of this "model protectorate," as it came to be known. In more spiteful terms Denmark was sometimes referred to as "Hitler's little canary."

Members of Hitler's fascist National Socialist Party, the Nazis, appeared everywhere after the invasion and during the occupation. The party was founded on the principle of German world dominance, including the eventual elimination of Jews, Communists and other "undesirables." As far as Danes were concerned, all Germans were one and the same, whether they were Nazis, the Gestapo (German secret police), storm-troopers (SS--special units of German military police) or Germans in the regular armed services.

During negotiations between the Danish government and the invaders, the "Jewish question" had not been a part of the discussions. The idea of singling out an ethnic group for special treatment was not compatible with the Danish spirit of community and equality. Therefore, Jews living in Denmark would continue to receive the same constitutional guarantees that were the right of all Danes. This was a radical departure from the usual policy in other occupied countries. Even the Germans realized this matter was potentially explosive and needed to be considered carefully if they wanted to keep negotiations going on an even keel.

At first Germany needed Denmark. Its geographic location was important as a base to transport soldiers and war materiel to the north where the Germans were occupying Norway. Food produced in Denmark was also a valuable addition to the limited German food supply. Thus this newly occupied country was ruled with a benign hand.

Although shocked by the lightning blitz of the invasion, it did not take long for most Danes to adapt to their new situation. On the surface, life appeared to change very little during the early years of the occupation. In fact, in comparison with what was taking place in all the other European countries which were being ground under the heel of Nazi oppression, Denmark fared remarkably well.

For the first three years of the occupation (1940-1943), problems between the two countries were settled in a business-like manner by means of the "policy of negotiation" which had been agreed upon by both sides. German soldiers behaved respectfully toward the Danish population. Unlike other occupied countries, there was enough food. Only coffee, butter, bread and sugar were rationed, along with tobacco and textiles, and even those items generally were available from friendly neighborhood merchants. Although the gas supply was limited, that was the major restriction on the otherwise almost normal lifestyle of the Danes. Germans confiscated some of the items usually found in stores, but paid promptly for whatever merchandise they bought, albeit payment was made with funds appropriated from local branches of the Danish National Bank which meant, in reality, that Danes were paying for German purchases. Cultural events continued with the Royal Theater featuring regular performances of the opera and the internationally famous Danish Royal Ballet.

Since Denmark was determined *not* to be involved in the war raging in Europe, co-existence with the enemy appeared to be the best means to that end. By maintaining their role as a "model protectorate," the Danes believed that under the circumstances they had the best of all worlds. Thus, from 1940 to 1943, Denmark succeeded in being a peaceful, productive nation, in spite of the fact the country was under the control of a hated foreign government.

The official state church of the country is Lutheran, with pastors being paid from public taxes. Early on, by the time Knud was fifteen years old, he found the strict conservative basis of Lutheranism not to his liking. While he did not leave the church, he no longer was a formal practitioner of the faith. To this day, however, he attributes his high standards regarding goodness, honesty and altruism as being based on the tenets of his early religious training.

Although most Danes are not avid churchgoers, they are tolerant of their neighbors' religious practices. So it was, during the first three years of the German occupation, the Jews in Denmark were treated exactly as they had been before--which was no differently from anyone else.

3

Jewish People
in Denmark

While life for Danish Jews went on in a relatively normal way, this was not true for many Jewish peoples elsewhere in Europe. Outright anti-Semitism surfaced and latent anti-Semitism became more apparent across the continent.

In the course of history almost no country has escaped the taint of anti-Semitism. Discrimination against Jews was demonstrated in hidden, subtle ways, but in many instances was government-sanctioned. During the Second World War, when countries were invaded and occupied by Hitler's armies, most citizens of these countries were already inured or indifferent to the inferior status accorded Jews or actively cooperated and participated in their harassment and roundup. A rare exception was Denmark, where the persecution of Jews has been nonexistent and outright opposition to anti-Semitism is part of the customs and heritage of the Danish people.

How did Jews come to live in Denmark? Why is the story of Danish Jews so different? The history of the Jewish community in Denmark is relatively brief, at least by comparison with the history of the Jews in much of the rest of Europe. They first arrived in Denmark in 1622, when King Christian IV invited some Portuguese Jews from Amsterdam and Hamburg to live in his country. Those Jews were welcomed because they were prosperous and had connections with international businesses, all of which would be good for Denmark.

The Danes' high regard for their Jewish neighbors is evidenced as far back as 1670, only decades after the arrival of the first Jews in the country, when a local police chief was fired from his job because he dared suggest that Denmark do what other countries did at the time--establish a ghetto where the Jews would be forced to live separately from other people.

At the end of the 17th century a few Jewish families from Germany were given the right to emigrate to Denmark and their arrival enlarged the Jewish community. The new immigrants were craftsmen who began opening their own small businesses. Later, Jews were granted permission to hold prayers in their homes and buy land for their own cemetery. As years went by they were granted additional privileges unheard of for Jews in other parts of the world: they did not have to live isolated in a ghetto and were allowed to manage their own affairs without government interference. The Danes were far ahead of their time in extending these civil rights to Jews.

By 1766 the Jews from Germany and northern Europe had established their own synagogue in Copenhagen. A small number of Danish Jews were even allowed to enroll in schools of higher learning, particularly medicine, although they were not permitted to actually get a medical degree or practice as doctors. The better-educated Jews sometimes converted to Christianity and became Lutherans in order to be eligible for occupations still denied to members of their faith.

In 1814 the Danish Parliament passed legislation making *all* racial and religious discrimination illegal. Jews were granted full Danish citizenship, and in 1849, with the end of the absolute monarchy when the country adopted its first free constitution, *all* citizens were granted religious freedom. This included Jews and others who were non-Lutherans.

In the latter part of the 19th century, Jewish influence proliferated. Jews played a pominent role in agricultural development, especially in dairy farming. Important companies like Bing & Grøndahl (porcelain) and the Tuborg Brewery were founded by Jews, giving them increased influence in the business world. Their talents were evident in art and music as well, where they made significant contributions to Danish culture. They were also patrons of the arts. A Jewish family, the Melchiors, housed famed Danish writer Hans Christian Andersen until his death in 1875. Coming from poverty, it is said he went to a Jewish school because it was free.

Because many Jews converted and others intermarried, the Jewish population in Denmark decreased somewhat, dropping from about 4,000 in the mid-1850s to 3,500 by 1900. Between 1900 and 1920, however, many Jews from Russia, Poland and the Baltic countries made their way to Denmark. They were escaping persecution and pogroms, the organized massacre of Jews in towns and villages all across Russia. Sometimes the pogroms were approved by the government and sometimes authorities looked the other way, but the result was the same--many Jews were again being forced to leave their homeland.

Unlike the Jews who had been living in Denmark for a long time, the 2,600 new immigrants were mostly poor, and each family usually had many children. Since Eastern European Jews were very knowledgeable about their religion and fervent about maintaining their culture, they helped keep the Jewish community in Denmark from disintegrating and forgetting its roots.

The various Jewish groups were brought together through the formation of a special organization within the Jewish community which served as a focal point for resolving friction. Adding to the cohesion, a community newspaper was published dealing with local Jewish news. When Nazism emerged in Germany, the paper printed articles about the problems besetting Jews there.

The European continent's first ominous rumblings of Hitler's anti-Semitism were felt in 1933 when the German government called for a boycott of all Jewish businesses in that country. Jews began trying to flee not only from Germany but also from Austria and Czechoslovakia, where Nazi presence was already being felt. The fate of fellow European Jews became a matter of great concern and a central committee was formed to help Jewish refugees get to Denmark. However, not all Danes were eager to increase the population during a time of economic hardship and unemployment. The government put guidelines and restraints into effect, strictly controlling the admission of refugees. In addition, Denmark had a long-standing policy of restricting *all* immigrants, and to admit any refugees required changes in the law.

Nonetheless, King Christian X (1876-1947), a good friend to the Jews, joined with the Danish government in making it clear that the Jews of Denmark were considered a part of the general population of the country. In a very visible and highly symbolic appearance on April 12, 1933, the King attended a service in the great synagogue of Copenhagen, which was celebrating its 100th anniversary. His visit was a message to the Germans that Jewish citizens in Denmark were highly regarded and respected.

Members of the Jewish community tried to warn the Danish public about the danger of the anti-Semitism rising in Germany. But even though Danes talked about the matter, there did not seem to be much real concern. Finally, after a Danish edition of the Portugese, anti-Semitic publication, *The Protocols of the Elders of Zion,* appeared in 1936, several Danish religious leaders spoke out against anti-Semitic literature. This was the first recognition of the increased threat against the Jews.

Even after November 9, 1938, the date of the infamous "Krystallnacht," when synagogues with their precious Torah scrolls and prayer books were burned, Jewish-owned businesses looted and trashed, 96 Jews killed, and over 1,000 Jewish homes, schools, hospitals and cemeteries destroyed in cities and towns all across Germany, some Danes still believed the reports that such incidents were only the result of "spontaneous outbursts" by the German people, rather than the officially government-orchestrated events they actually were.

Because of immigration restrictions, as late as 1939 relatively few Jewish refugees managed to escape to Denmark, compared with the numbers able to get to Holland, France and Great Britain. Only about 5,000 Jewish refugees were allowed to enter Denmark and most of them on temporary visas.

Before the invasion and occupation in 1940, Denmark and Germany had an on-going business relationship with good commercial ties that the Danes did not wish to jeopardize. They had no desire to call any undue attention to their country which might result in a negative impact on trade.

Even after the invasion, German assurances to the Danish government included the statement that "...the Germans did not intend to disturb the territorial integrity nor the political independence of the Kingdom of Denmark." This meant the Danish people could expect to find few, if any, changes in their lives, as long as they cooperated. The Danes skillfully used that principle as their guide when negotiating with the Germans about the many issues that arose because of the occupation.

At the time of the German occupation in 1940, Denmark had a population of some four and one-half million people, including about 8,000 Jews. The Jewish population was comprised of the various groups already mentioned: long-time Danish-Jewish families, Russian immigrants of the early 1900s and refugees from Germany who had managed to get into the country. There also were two relatively small groups of foreign Jews who were stranded in Denmark at the moment of invasion and occupation: some were students learning farming techniques they hoped to use in Palestine, and others were children, known as the *Aliyah Children*, who were passing through Denmark en route, they thought, to Palestine, the homeland of their dreams. Happily for all the young people involved, the Danish government and the Danish people regarded "Danish Jews" and "Jews in Denmark" as one and the same, placing both groups under the protection of crown and country. Others were spouses and children of mixed marriages who, whether they thought of themselves as Jews or not, realized the Germans might think of them that way.

The fate of Danish Jews was linked with the fate of Denmark; Jews would not be treated differently from any other Danes. As long as the government insisted the status of Denmark's Jews mattered only to the people and government of Denmark, their security lay in the government's integrity and ability to protect them. The Jewish community had to have total confidence in the government.

For their part, it was understood the Jews would not take part in any action that might weaken the Danish government's position in its continuing negotiations with the Germans. More importantly, it meant Jews would not act in any way that might bring even the matter of Jewish existence into discussions with the enemy.

"There is no Jewish problem in Denmark" became the standard response by Danes whenever the matter was brought up by the Germans. As far as the Danes were concerned, this was true--there was no Jewish problem in Denmark because Jews in Denmark were treated just like everyone else.

The year 1940 passed with no threat and little change for Denmark's Jews. But their concerns increased each time the Danish government was forced to make any compromise or concession in the on-going negotiations with the Nazis. In June, 1941, the Germans pressured the Danish government to pass a law which permitted the arrest of some 300 Danish Communists, resulting in the eventual internment of 100 of them in a Danish camp at Horserød, some thirty miles north of Copenhagen. The law struck fear into the hearts of many Jews. It meant the Danish government had agreed to allow certain exceptions to the principles of human rights and individual freedom that were so highly prized. If this marked a beginning of the erosion of political policy, the Jews knew they could be next.

4

The Young Knud

It is now almost sixty years since the young Knud Dyby witnessed the invasion and occupation of Denmark. Today he lives in a small town on the California coast, north of San Francisco. A former yachtsman, printer, inventor, public speaker and somewhat of a philosopher, he is in his eighties, sturdy and tall with blue eyes and ruddy complexion. From his living room, he can see the sparkling waters of San Francisco Bay. "I have to be near the water," he says, "even if I can't go sailing the way I did when I was young in Denmark."

Dyby was born on March 28, 1915, in the small town of Vorup, just outside the city of Randers on the Jutland Peninsula. Denmark had remained neutral during World War I (1914-1918), but throughout the war and for a time afterward only basic necessities were available. Dyby recalls, "I grew up on coffee, Danish pastry, potatoes and gravy. Times were hard during the First World War, when I was a child."

His family was close-knit, as Danish families are, and Knud fondly remembers his parents and his grandparents and great-grandparents as well, who all lived in neighboring towns in Jutland. Living in a land of islands and a peninsula as they did, it is natural that the Danes have been a seafaring people since the days of the Vikings, and Dyby's family was no exception.

My grandfather, my uncles and my father were yachtsmen. They did not sail fiberglass boats with roller-reefing jibs and efficient motors, like today's boats. They sailed in boats made of pine or oak that we propelled with a large oar when the wind died, and we maintained them ourselves. My memories of my early years are all connected to the sea and fjords.

Young Dyby thrived in the security of warm relationships with his father, Emil Olsen, mother, Dagmar, and younger brother, Sven. Emil Olsen, a typographer who eventually owned his own print shop and advertising company, was an expert gymnast and had been a member of the 1912 Danish Olympic team. At age seventy-five he still rode his scooter, often loaded down with flowers and bags of fruit from his garden. (Knud took the name Dyby after World War II. "I grew up with the long hyphenated name Dyring-Olsen, and then after living with fictitious names from 1943-45, I just decided to change it, and on May 31, 1945, I made it official.")

Knud often heard the story of how, when he was a baby, his father took him aboard the family boat and put him in a sling under the deck. If he got restless and cried, his father gave him a sip of *Aquavit*, the national Danish drink, to quiet him. When he was a little boy, he often walked with his father down to the harbor.

We both loved the water and we liked to watch the schooners load or unload supplies of coal and lumber and fodder. We also watched the fishermen mending their nets, but mostly we looked at yachts, wishing we could own or sail them.

Although the family was not well off and lived in a one-bedroom apartment, Knud's parents enrolled him in a private school, the Charlotte LaCour School, because it was only a block away from home. The school had the reputation for being the "rich kids' school," and Knud still remembers his feelings about being poor because his mother had to mend the holes on the elbows of his sweaters, in contrast to his schoolmates' fine new clothing. And he remembers how hard it was for him to ask his father for "one or two crowns" to buy a gift for friends when invited to birthday parties in their elegant homes. "Sometimes I was invited to stay overnight with friends, but because our apartment was so small I could not reciprocate."

Before long the family moved to a house, called "Villa Home," surrounded by lovely gardens. Knud's feelings soon reflected his change of status and he became more secure and self-reliant. Like most young Danes, he and his new friends read Bernhard Severin Ingemann's stories about romantic, swashbuckling heroes. They avidly read magazines, newspapers and books that described the arctic adventures of Danes Knud Rasmussen, Hvidbjerg and Knuth, and Norwegians Amundsen and Nansen. "My father had me pick up books about the Greenland and polar adventurers and I read them all." The boys fantasized about becoming mighty warriors and explorers. They swam in the nearby river and the fjord.

> *Actually, the fjord was supposed to be fresh water, but it wasn't all that fresh as we sometimes would swim into dead pigs and other unhealthy remnants from a nearby slaughter house. The fjord water was better for eels and pike than swimming. Because my family couldn't afford an automobile, it was a special treat when friends invited us to go with them to the beaches, forty or fifty miles from town.*

Dyby concedes that he wasn't much of a student. He often arrived at school with the wrong books and was seldom prepared for the day's lessons, but he says he learned fast, and "I was an expert in copying from my nearest classmate." He also spent a lot of time being punished by having to stand outside the classroom among the coats hanging in the hallway. He remembers the times when he neglected to do his homework and was required to appear with it after school at the private homes of his teachers.

The family moved again to even better living quarters, and young Knud and his father became the happy owners of a small sailboat named *Pust* (Puff). After a few cruises with the Sea Scouts on their boat, *Electra,* followed by a yachting apprenticeship on a bigger craft belonging to the Randers Sejlclub (Yachting Club), 17

Knud at the rudder of his small sailboat "Pust".

year old Knud earned a certificate giving him the right to navigate the waters around Denmark, including the Øresund, the sound between Denmark and Sweden that was to become the escape route of World War II. His boat became the love of his life (". . . besides dating pretty girls") and by the time he was 21 years old he had won 22 silver cups for sailing.

In spite of his lackadaisical academic endeavors, at age 18 Dyby completed the formal schooling required by Danish law. He then apprenticed as a printer and typographer. "The work really interested me. The shop was small, with only three others, so we had to do everything--from handling the customers to the finished book binding and delivery." At the same time he enrolled in a five-year technical high school, something many young Danes did to continue their education. The evening classes at the Randers' school were compulsory and with the tutelage of good teachers Dyby became a "star" in graphic arts.

In 1935, just before his 20th birthday, Knud Dyby, as required, appeared before a Danish military commission to fulfill his compulsory service in the army or navy. With a twinkle in his eye, he relates the following story:

> *They usually wanted handsome fellows to serve as the King's Guard. It must have been a bad year for good looks because they chose me to serve in the Royal Guard Regiment. Only two are chosen from each county to serve in that Regiment so that was a high honor. Friends and family all over town wanted to know what you were "taken" to become; to be chosen for the Royal Guard was something to brag about. Everyone was exuberant, and when I told my old grandfather, a former infantry soldier and a bearer of the standard, he had tears in his eyes.*

Knud is proud of his service as a Guardsman. He remembers his handsome uniform and marching down the streets of Copenhagen with his unit, a marching band playing and spectators waving.

Besides receiving the usual military instruction, Guardsmen

Dyby as a guardsman in red tunic outside the barracks.

also were given special training in guarding the King and his family and the castles where the royal family stayed.

> *We lived at the Guards' Barracks at Rosenborg Castle, while every three days we spent twenty four hours at the various castles -- Amalienborg, Rosenborg, Marselisborg and Fredensborg, and on special occasions, Christiansborg. I have wonderful memories of the times I lifted one of King Christian's grandchildren up to him while he sat on his big horse. The King was not a man who smiled often, but then he would smile, just like grandfathers smile all over the world for their grandchildren.*

Knud served in the Royal Guard in 1937 and was called up again in 1938 when the Germans occupied the Sudetenland, an area in Czechoslovakia bordering Germany, which they claimed was mostly inhabited by their countrymen. Because there did not appear to be any threat to Denmark at that time, Knud did not have to stay in service very long. But he has fond recollections of being stationed in a beautiful seaside village twenty miles north of Copenhagen where he and other Guardsmen were invited into the home of Karen Blixen, one of Denmark's foremost writers and author of *Out of Africa*. She served them sherry and told them about the stories she was writing. Shortly after that assignment Dyby returned to a job in the printing trade in Copenhagen. "My uncle and aunt lived across the street from where I was staying, and I still remember what a splendid cook she was!"

Although Germany was beginning to flex its military muscle, and in spite of the threatening clouds of war in the rest of Europe, life in insular Denmark was peaceful and good.

Knud Dyby's parents, Emil and Dagmar Olsen, in the living room of their home in Randers, Jutland.

5

A Policeman

The quiet life that Denmark had known changed with the German invasion and occupation beginning on the morning of April 9, 1940. Shortly after, Dyby, who had been visiting his parents in Randers on that fateful day, returned to his job as a typographer in Copenhagen.

As the occupation progressed, the Germans arbitrarily confiscated much of the raw material used by Danish factories, including paper and paper products. This in turn affected the printing industry, leaving little work for a printer, and Knud decided to look for other employment. He saw a newspaper advertisement placed by the police department; Danish authorities, still in control of local police forces, were looking for recruits. Former Guardsmen were highly regarded, and on June 24, 1940, his application was accepted.

His first assignment as an aspiring policeman started within the month, in the town of Horsens, in Jutland. The main duty of the local police, according to Dyby, was to "... keep the restless population from performing acts of anti-German behavior, such as personal attacks on the military." This included preventing sabotage in German-controlled factories where Danes unwillingly worked for the enemy.

While working in Horsens, Dyby received commendations for rescuing a family from a burning house and also for stopping a runaway horse and carriage. He enjoyed police work and came to respect his fellow officers.

For several intervals in 1940 and 1941, he was sent from Horsens to Toftlund, close to the German border, to assist the police there because of trouble in the area. It was in Toftlund that Dyby became involved in his first resistance activity. An important function of the police was to track English planes flying over Denmark en route to bomb German targets; this information was then reported to police headquarters. But Dyby and other policemen found that Nazi intelligence officers were intercepting the reports with the consequence that German military authorities were able to warn their troops and anti-aircraft weapons were being deployed against the English. It did not take long for Dyby and his colleagues to adjust their reports; several times a night when they heard the backfire of a truck going up a steep hill they reported it as an overflight of English planes. The Germans never caught on and their anti-aircraft gunners got less and less sleep.

In April 1942, Dyby requested and was granted a transfer to Frederiksberg, a district in Copenhagen. Following completion of his training at the police academy in Hellerup, outside of Copenhagen, he became a fully qualified police officer in July 1942. Dyby lived in a very nice apartment, one that even had steel plates inside the doors to deter forced entry. This was necessary since his visitors frequently included saboteurs and other resistance workers. If one of his underground connections were arrested by the Gestapo, Dyby had to be extra careful. This involved entering his apartment, pistol in hand, and searching the place. Then he would lock the door, climb out the window and make his way to an attic storage space. There he could sleep peacefully on a cot, knowing that even if the Germans broke into his apartment they would not find him.

As a member of the police department, Dyby had access to stacks of illegal newspapers. The papers were meant to be discarded, but Dyby distributed them to anyone who dared to take them.

> *All I had to do was to listen to them talk with disgust and anger about the enemy and the occupation and I could decide how eager they were to get a copy of one of the papers and then test their willingness to distribute some to their friends.*

Dyby remembers that the police had to stand back and not interfere when the Germans arrested a suspected Danish saboteur or troublemaker, but after their release these same Danes were an important source of information about treatment they had received at the hands of the Gestapo or German police.

In essence, the police were being called upon to perform a fine balancing act. On one hand, they were required to keep the peace and maintain order, or at least make it appear that way. Daily instructions from the German-controlled government were handed down to the local precincts, ordering them to stop Danes from attacking military posts and factories. "On the other hand," says Dyby, "we hardly looked at the instructions, but we had to carefully avoid our few fellow officers who felt it was their duty to do exactly as they were told."

It was not long before Dyby made contact with members or leaders of such resistance groups as *Holger Danske* (named for a mythic figure who was to come to Denmark's aid when the nation was in dire need), *Frit Danmark* (Free Denmark), *Dansk Samling* (Danish Unification), *Studenternes Efterretningstjeneste* (The Students' Intelligence Service), and others. The Danes who started to help Dyby by distributing underground papers often expanded their aid to include hiding people from the Gestapo, donating clothing, food and money, even contributing an occasional gun to the cause. Some became active, full-fledged members of one or another of the resistance groups.

Knud inspects a bomb crater outside Horsens, Jutland, in 1942.

6

Early Resistance to the Germans

At first there was little resistance to the occupation, secret or otherwise, even though the majority of Danes were anti-German and especially anti-Nazi.

In April 1940, the men in the Danish army were mostly untrained recruits scattered in posts around the country. Until ordered to stop, many fought a courageous but futile, brief fight against the overwhelming enemy force. Royal Danish Guardsmen fought bravely when the invaders attacked the palace at Amalienborg where King Christian was staying, but the Germans quickly called a halt to the action because they wanted the King to remain on the throne as a figurehead of the country.

Looking back at history, there is divided opinion among Danes today regarding whether surrender was the right thing to do. Many agree with the action which was taken: that strong resistance at the time of the invasion would have meant great hardship and would have resulted in enormous casualties to the population. On the other hand, others believe that the "mutual negotiation treaty" the Danes agreed to when the occupation started, was closer to *collaboration* than cooperation and therefore was not the honorable solution.

In the early days of the occupation there were only a few isolated pockets of resistance to the enemy, resistance which was passive and unarmed. Some of the protests were actually directed toward the Danish government, rather than the invaders, because many Danes thought their government had yielded too quickly. Even some local Danish police forces were called names by the few resisters.

All agree that if the Danish people had resisted and been overpowered by the Germans, as they almost surely would have, the Jews of Denmark would immediately have been rounded up and deported to concentration camps.

The small wave of passive resistance that began early in the occupation gave rise to a ground swell of patriotism and national spirit. Crowds of Copenhagen residents gathered in the morning to cheer King Christian as he set out from Amalienborg Palace to begin his daily ride on horseback around the city. A German soldier, amazed at seeing the King in public without bodyguards, asked, "Who protects him?" A young Danish woman standing nearby, proudly replied, "We all do."

A popular legend has it that as a show of support for his Jewish subjects, King Christian wore the Star of David, but that did not actually happen. As recorded, in the first three years of the occupation (1940-1943), before the threatened deportation, Danish Jews were treated the same as other Danes. They did not have to wear the six-pointed insignia that Jews in other occupied countries were forced to wear, yet the legend persists that during those years Danish Jews were made to wear the star and in defiance of the Nazis the King also wore one. The story is believable because of the Danish royal family's strong support for all Danes.

During the early days of the occupation Danish flags and pennants flew from many buildings. Many citizens wore *Kongemaerket*, the initials of King Christian X, on their lapels, and students wore red, white and blue caps, the colors of the British Air Force. Danes gathered all across the country to sing patriotic folk songs. The "cold shoulder" treatment was a popular tactic of passive resistance, a way of simply ignoring the presence of the enemy. And of course Germans were not invited into Danish homes.

But the Danes became increasingly unhappy about food shortages and mounting restrictions which were imposed on their daily lives by the Germans. As the war in Europe escalated and the occupation wore on, the resistance grew larger and stronger.

King Christian X rides through the streets of Copenhagen.

Beginning in the summer of 1942, there were more and more acts of sabotage against the occupying force. Strikes in factories were commonplace and became a unifying symbol for the Danish people. The strikes became a way of expressing the national shame Danes felt because their country had surrendered to the invasion with so little resistance. The protests continued even though the strikes always were followed by heavy-handed German reprisals.

By 1943, after three years of occupation, the resistance movement had grown very fast and the police were in a special position to be helpful to the cause. Not all police chose to be involved, but many did and managed small-scale incidents of sabotage. Dyby recalls driving around with some colleagues on patrol in his police car and throwing bricks through the windows of an office building used by the Nazis, then reporting back to their station that "some unknown irresponsible individuals had taken part in an act of anti-German behavior."

Recalling one particular incident brings a broad smile to Dyby's face:

> I was sent to a local theater where it was reported that some young "hoodlums" were causing a disturbance by trying to disrupt the showing of a German-approved movie. I did not want to arrest the young people, who were obviously resisting in their own way, but I was a policeman and I had to do something. I took the movie reel, handed one end of the film to a member of the group and ordered them all to leave. When they ran away, I put my shoe lightly on the film as it dragged along the floor, scratching it thoroughly so it could not be shown again. I reported back to my superiors that a gang had destroyed the film.

The police were given names of Danes hired to guard factories. Just before an act of sabotage was to take place, police, with pistols in hand, would persuade the guards to disappear or look the other way while the sabotage was going on. "We did as much as we could to make life miserable for the Germans," he remembers, with satisfaction.

32

In 1943, while still in police uniform, Dyby occasionally was sent out by himself on his bicycle to patrol a district on the edge of town. He remembers,

It was strange. The world was at war, terrible events were taking place in so many other countries, and there I was on bicycle patrol. I would check the doors of shops and factories to be sure they were locked, but I was on duty at three o'clock in the morning and everything was dark and silent. I was bored and it was a very disquieting feeling. Occasionally I would stop at a local bakery where they were already baking their bread for the day with the door open so they could get some fresh air. I'd knock and they always gave me a cup of coffee and maybe a roll and we would sit there and talk about the war. Sometimes now when I can't fall asleep at night, I can see myself on my bike riding around the district. I was so tired and sleepy and lonesome and nothing was happening. Sometimes I would sit down on a bench or even the stairs to a house with my bike alongside and rest a little while. I thought how absolutely ridiculous it was for me to be out on a bicycle riding around the back roads where nothing was happening. Of course, if something had happened, it would have been different, but nothing ever did.

Matters came to a head August 29, 1943, when Dr. Werner Best, the representative of German authority in Denmark, was called to Berlin and instructed by Hitler to "be tough" with the Danes. Martial law was declared and the resulting emergency decree imposed many restrictions, including an early curfew, prohibitions against strikes, and the forbidding of more than five people from gathering in one place. Firearms and explosives were confiscated. Most infuriating and humiliating of all were the tribunals established in which Danish citizens themselves were to deal with violators and impose punishment as ordered by the Nazis. Captured saboteurs were immediately condemned to death. Part of the new plan was to include replacing Danish government leaders with new Danish personnel who were likely to go along with German demands.

On September 23, 1943, The Freedom Council was organized. Composed of leaders of various underground groups, the Council's goal was to develop and broaden means to harass the enemy and thwart new decrees. There was no question of unity of agreement on this issue among the many groups represented in The Council.

In response to the state of emergency orders issued by the Germans, King Christian X declared himself a political prisoner and refused to leave the palace. The Danish cabinet resigned, followed by Parliament voting to dissolve itself. The Danish navy deliberately scuttled the remaining ships in its fleet. The Germans immediately assumed complete control over the government of Denmark.

For the time being, the *Wehrmacht*, the armed forces of Nazi Germany, controlled Denmark. Dr. Best, until then the highest ranking German in the country, was replaced by the *Wehrmacht* commander, General von Hanneken, and the Germans promptly moved to take harsh actions against the underground.

Dr. Best sent an infamous telegram to his superiors in Berlin, urging the immediate roundup of the Jews. His motives for doing this remain unclear as previously he had agreed with the "soft" handling of the "Jewish problem"; perhaps he thought he could ingratiate himself to Hitler. Then he had second thoughts and attempted to delay the roundup, but by that time Hitler was incensed with the acts of sabotage he blamed on the Jews and ordered the action to proceed.

Earlier, a hundred Danes who were members of the Danish Communist Party had been interned in the concentration camp at Horserød north of Copenhagen. Now the Nazis executed a young member of the resistance. A wave of outrage rolled across the nation.

The Jews were next. By the end of September 1943, it became apparent that in spite of all that had been done to protect them, the Jewish people of Denmark would face the same fate as had overtaken Jews elsewhere in occupied countries of Europe.

The Nazis were confident they controlled the government and the police. However, they were misguided in the belief they were in complete control of coastal waters. They would soon find this was not the case.

An act of sabotage stopped this factory from producing goods for the German war machine.

36

7

The Underground

Historically, there had been tensions between Danes and Germans along their common border at the base of the Jutland peninsula. This dated back to Danish struggles with north German cities early in the 13th century. In 1864, after the Dano-Prussian War, the two duchies of Schleswig and Holstein that had long been a part of the Danish realm were lost to Prussia. While Holstein was populated by German peoples, Schleswig was a borderland where the two peoples mingled. The loss of these two duchies inspired a deep resentment among Danes toward their German neighbors.

After the German invasion in 1940, it was only a matter of time until active resistance to the occupation was organized. Underground groups sprang up all over the country, instigating as much sabotage as they could, and before long the resistance movement became a powerful force working against the German occupiers.

There were many small groups of resisters working independently of each other, but all had the same goal--to harass and defy the Germans and to resist in every possible way the regulations imposed on their country by the Nazis. Factories making parts for German industry were damaged, sometimes as a result of saboteurs entering factories, machine gun in one hand, explosives in the other and daringly placing bombs where machinery would be damaged. Bridges and sections of the railroad which carried German troops through Denmark to German-occupied Norway were blown up. Some of the younger men in the resistance, courageous but often reckless in their attacks, robbed German officers of their pistols while others stole trucks from German drivers, right off the streets of Copenhagen.

Although only a small percentage of Danes actively participated in the underground movement, assisting them was a larger network of Danish citizens who helped in the cause. These men and women helpers did whatever they could to assist the active workers by passing information, getting equipment and arms, distributing papers and by finding safe houses for those who were engaged in the dangerous work of resistance.

On September 29, 1943, when it became known that the Germans intended to round up the Jews in Denmark and deport them, Danes decided they had had enough. Those who had been working bravely with the underground in resisting the Germans now assumed a new and broader role. Even those Danes who had passively accepted the occupation came to the defense of their Jewish countrymen. All of Denmark appeared to be working together to help the Nazi victims reach safety.

Knud Dyby was a helper. He was proud of his Danish heritage and angry at having to live under the thumb of the hated Germans. As a Christian he was not personally acquainted with many Jews, but he knew right from wrong and was aware that any Jew who was rounded up and deported would certainly end up in one of the infamous German concentration camps, about which members of the underground were just beginning to learn.

It was through the underground press that Danes learned about Hitler's genocidal plan to kill the Jews of Europe. The fires of Krystallnacht, the roundup of Jewish men, women and children in other occupied countries, and the existence of the infamous concentration camps--all were publicized in the underground press. Dyby was an avid reader, securing the papers from friends who knew his feelings, and soon he was actively involved in the resistance by helping to distribute the underground newspapers. Some Danes were too scared to even have an illegal paper in their possession, while others accepted gladly and went one step further by helping in the distribution. In Knud's case, his activity led to much broader involvement which eventually included supplying some of the newsprint used in the printing process. Others helped hide people from the Gestapo, contributed weapons, or donated food or money to resistance groups, while still others became active members of such groups.

Obtaining explosives and ammunition was a high priority and that was one place Dyby could help. Using his own money as well as raising money from friends, Dyby obtained guns and hand grenades which he passed on to the underground. He says, "The army and navy depots were very helpful in getting guns for us. And more than once guns that had been stolen from Danish depots were given to freedom fighters. We also got guns in 'drops' from Allied planes. And sometimes German soldiers, on their way to other fronts, would 'lose' their pistols for 200 Kroner (Danish crowns). It really does not take many guns to make sabotage. One for each." As an afterthought, Dyby remembers, "Keep in mind that during the occupation those in the resistance never, never *stole* anything. We merely *organized* what we needed or wanted for what we considered a good purpose. And until the police were rounded up on September 19, 1944, police officers could own handguns and therefore 'organized' more than one."

With his military training Dyby taught many of the young volunteers how to use firearms. Much of the planning and careful handling of the weapons was done in the dead of night, right under the nose of the enemy. "It was extremely important not to be caught with a weapon, so they always had to be hidden."

Often a resistance group had a specialty such as sabotaging factories, damaging railroads and railroad equipment, or investigating (and eliminating) Danish informers to the Gestapo, the German secret police. Other groups provided money, weapons and safe houses where the resisters could be securely hidden from the enemy. "Safe" houses were an important part of the underground movement because it was vital for resistance workers to have places where they knew they could safely hide. Such houses were rarely houses--more often they were apartments or just a room in a friendly private home. For a time Dyby lived in a 5th floor apart-

One of many acts of sabotage carried out by resistance groups to slow the transport of goods bound for Germany.

ment. He remembers:

> *When I found that an informer, a pro-Nazi Dane, had*
> *moved into an apartment on the 3rd floor, I notified the*
> *'proper' people in the underground. Soon the informer*
> *found all of his furniture out on the sidewalk. It had not*
> *been taken downstairs on the elevator. It had been thrown*
> *out of his apartment window. He left and never came*
> *back.*

Dyby, still in his uniform as a police officer but actively supporting the resistance, frequently was just a step ahead of the Gestapo. In one case, he and a fellow resistance worker named Henning Petersen were to meet someone who claimed to be able to get weapons from the Germans. Petersen was the manager at a fashionable Copenhagen restaurant whose job included making reservations for guests. As Dyby and Petersen approached the meeting place, Dyby noted the presence of some suspicious looking people and suggested to Petersen, "Let's skip the meeting," and they left. Shortly afterwards, Dyby learned that when Petersen returned to the restaurant he was shot and killed--apparently because he often refused to make reservations for German officers.

Dyby always found some place to stay, even after a *quisling* had given his name to the German commander, General von Hanneken. (Vidkun Quisling was a Norwegian official and politician who actively collaborated with the Germans in their conquest of Norway. His name became synonymous with *traitor*. After the war he was shot by the Norwegians.) Such informers as the one who reported Dyby for taking part in anti-German activities were rare, but there were enough to make life hazardous and uncertain.

After he was reported to the Germans, Dyby's apartment was no longer safe and he spent the rest of the war on the move. Sometimes he was able to stay in one place for weeks at a time and sometimes he had to move almost every day. Yet he never was without a place of sanctuary, frequently with people he did not know. Every class of Danish society, from ordinary citizens to members of Denmark's nobility, helped hide resistance workers.

Besides moving from place to place, Dyby changed his name whenever he thought the Gestapo was getting too close. Pedersen, Carlsen and Berg were some of his aliases. Because of his interest in printing, Dyby was able to pose as a photographer which gave him more freedom to move around.

Contact between resistance workers was kept to a minimum. "It was just better not to know who was doing what," recalls Dyby. Messages were delivered in person or through a trusted third party, and telephone calls between contacts were brief and carefully discreet.

The Germans responded to acts of sabotage by blowing up apartment and office buildings and even part of the Danes' cherished Tivoli Gardens, the amusement park and gardens located in the heart of Copenhagen. Unfortunately, more than a few innocent Danish bystanders were killed in these acts of German counter-sabotage.

When the Nazis got too close, underground workers smuggled the most-wanted resisters and saboteurs out of the country to Sweden. This was done with the help of sympathetic local fishermen who got them across the Øresund, the sound or waterway between Denmark and Sweden. Knud Dyby helped make the necessary arrangements for some of them, personally going to the harbor to seek out a helpful skipper.

Aage, a fishing skipper friend of Dyby's, had a special way of duping the Germans in the Navy Patrol, whose main purpose was to be sure that nothing illegal was going on in the waters around Denmark. When Patrol members would board his boat, Aage always offered them some good Danish bacon he kept in his cabin. Then, in a friendly way, he would ask whether they would like some fish when he returned from his fishing trip. The Germans were happy to give him their location so they could get the fish. Aage used the information to avoid the Patrol when he had something (or someone) on board that he did not want inspected.

There was one place where the rescuers did not have to fear the

Patrol. One of the main refuse dumps of Copenhagen was at Amager, close to the Kastrup Fort which was manned by German troops. The fort is on a hilltop, and the dump on low meadowy terrain right on the coast of the Sound. A few miles east lies the island of Saltholm, a flat, grass-covered meadow. The waters around Saltholm are on the shallow side and can only be used by boats with drafts of two to four feet. Consequently, large German patrol boats could not approach the island if they did not want to get grounded.

Some of the fishing skippers of Kastrup were very active in the rescues and resistance, and many refugees were transported directly from Kastrup Harbor or Saltholm over to the Swedish coast, south of Malmö and Landskrona. Also, many boats from the Swedish side picked up refugees in the vicinity of Saltholm. The personnel at the dump were helping the underground. When they had an important departure, and the wind was cooperating, the dump workers would start a good fire from wet material, with the result that the Germans on the fort were surrounded by a heavy, smelly smoke cloud which completely obstructed the view of the dump area--and the illegal activity.

A pattern developed that was repeated all over the country. First, Danish resisters carried out acts of sabotage against the occupiers. After each incident, more and more enemy soldiers would appear on the streets, followed by German counter-attacks such as the one on the treasured Tivoli Gardens. The final step often was a counter-strike by the Danes which would hurt production for the Germans. Local town and city police, who were Danes, were under great pressure because they were supposed to arrest the saboteurs and turn them over to the Germans, but most were not about to betray their countrymen, and a few were even actively cooperating in the resistance. At the same time, the Danish people tried to persuade their government to stop giving in to the enemy's threats and demands for increased cooperation.

It should be noted that although a few Jews, acting as individuals and motivated by Danish pride, became involved in the resistance movement, most of the Jewish people living in Denmark did not take an organized part in the underground. During the first three years of the occupation, leaders of the Jewish community believed the best course for Danish Jews was to "lay low" and be as unobtrusive and inconspicuous as possible. They prophetically felt that anything that might call attention to their people would be harmful in the long run.

8

The Roundup

By August of 1943, when it became apparent that resistance to the occupation was increasing and cooperation with the Danish government was almost non-existent, the Germans concluded they were no longer obliged to tread lightly when it came to treatment of Denmark's Jews.

In 1943, the Jewish New Year of Rosh Hashanah, one of the holiest days in the Jewish calendar, fell on October 1st. In the twisted minds of Hitler and Heinrich Himmler, his chief of the Gestapo, this would be a most appropriate day to activate the secret plan to round up and deport the Jews to Nazi concentration camps.

In September 1943, Georg F. Duckwitz, the German in charge of his country's shipping operations in Denmark, received secret instructions from the Nazis to have four cargo ships available so that all of the Danish Jews could be transported in one fell swoop. Duckwitz, however, was *not* sympathetic to the roundup plan. While he had joined the Nazi Party in 1932, hoping to rebuild a stronger Germany after the devastation of the First World War, an increasing distaste for Nazism impelled him to resign from the party in 1935, when he became chief accountant for the Hamburg-American Shipping Line. The expertise in international shipping he gained from this position was the background for his being sent to Copenhagen in 1939 as the maritime consultant to the German Embassy.

Now, at enormous personal risk, Duckwitz passed information about the roundup to Danish political leader Hans Hedtoft, who in turn advised the leaders of the Jewish community. Duckwitz also contacted a trusted friend, the German naval commander in Copenhagen, and urged him to "keep his eyes closed" to impending sea transports. In addition, Duckwitz made a hurried trip to Stockholm where he contacted government officials to persuade the Swedes to intervene directly with Germany. He also urged Sweden to prepare for the arrival of 8,000 refugees.

Stockholm responded by sending a telegram to Berlin asking that the plan to arrest Danish Jews be canceled. As Duckwitz anticipated, the request was ignored, but Sweden opened her borders to the escapees.

Incredibly, even at that late date, some Jewish leaders found the warning hard to believe, but recent raids on Jewish offices and businesses in which lists of names were confiscated, convinced them to take the matter seriously.

In the early hours of September 29, 1943, the synagogue in Copenhagen was only sparsely filled with worshipers when Rabbi Marcus Melchior, Acting Chief Rabbi in Copenhagen, announced to those present that the Germans intended to arrest all Jews on Rosh Hashanah. The Nazis knew that Jewish families would be gathering in their homes for the traditional celebration of the New Year holiday. Rabbi Melchior's tone commanded immediate attention as he told the congregation,

> *The situation is very serious. We must take action immediately. You must leave the synagogue now and contact all relatives, friends and neighbors you know who are Jewish and tell them what I have told you. You must also speak to your Christian friends and ask them to warn any Jews they know. You must do this immediately, within the next few minutes, so that two or three hours from now everyone will know what is happening. By nightfall we must all be in hiding.*

The sacred Torahs had already been hidden by Lutheran clergymen in the crypt of Trinity Church, a few blocks from the synagogue. Like their ancestors in many another country, the Jews fled from the synagogue and raced to spread the word. Rabbi Melchior also fled.

The Jews trusted Duckwitz and knew the message was not a hoax. The warning gave Jews and their friends time to prepare a plan of escape and permitted a precious few days to build up the exodus organizations about to be run by amateurs without previous experience in this illegal work.

The news about the planned raid spread like wildfire throughout the city. Jews not only warned other Jews, but as Rabbi Melchior had advised, they also told their trusted Christian friends and neighbors, knowing they would pass the word. Because there was fear that telephone lines might be tapped, and indeed Copenhagen's telephone service *was* temporarily disconnected by the Nazis, the message was passed mainly from person to person and family to family.

At this crucial point the Danish people responded promptly and wholeheartedly by offering help and sanctuary to their Jewish compatriots. This included Danes who previously had been reluctant to do anything that might have angered the Germans. Now they understood the time had come to draw the line. It was obvious to every Dane that the decision by the Germans to round up the Jews was not based on economic need or military strategy. Persecuting and deporting an innocent group of people would not help the Germans build a better economy or increase their chances of winning the war. The Danes knew the Nazis looked at the roundup not only as a means of venting frustration but also as a necessary action to bolster their diminishing authority.

The Germans underestimated the will of the Danes. The order to round up the Jews angered the Danish people in a way that not even the restrictions on their civil liberties, or the many acts of Nazi retaliation, or the arrest and murder of underground patriots, or food shortages had angered them. It is said that Danes by nature are such a law-abiding people that even in the middle of the night without a car in sight practically nobody crosses the street until the traffic signal says "walk." But the order to round up their Jewish neighbors brought about a change in psyche. These dutiful and peaceful people now became united in their determination to defy the orders of the enemy. *"Det kan man ikke,"* or *"Det kan du ikke vaere bekendt,"* roughly translated, "That is not acceptable," were expressions long used by Danes, and those were their feelings about the impending roundup.

Where did the Jews go? They went everywhere and anywhere--into the homes of friends and total strangers. They disappeared into Protestant churches, and they became guests in summer cottages and hotels. Hospital beds suddenly filled with an influx of "sick" people. Others fled the city to find refuge on farms and in the woods. Jews simply *vanished*.

Before the roundup, the Germans had confiscated copies of membership lists from the Jewish Community Center in Copenhagen. The lists included names and addresses of most of the Jews living in the city. In addition, during the early years of the occupation, the Nazis had searched through telephone books and other directories, compiling lists of Jewish names. Almost all of Denmark's Jews lived in the capital city, so gathering the names was an easy task.

Late in the night of September 29, 1943, a large German transport ship, the *Wartheland,* docked in Copenhagen Harbor, ready to take aboard the targeted Jews. At the same time, the harbor was cordoned off in anticipation of loading the victims on board ship.

Two days later, just after midnight, October 1st, Gestapo commandos and the special police spread throughout the city to start their hunt. All through the night they roamed Copenhagen in trucks, banging on doors and raiding houses where Jews lived. They found very few at home. Of Denmark's approximately 8,000 Jews, only 284 were captured that night, some of them too old or too ill to go into hiding. These were put aboard the German ship and transported the next day. By the time the roundup was officially completed, three weeks later, an additional 252 Jews were found and deported by train.

When the Swedish government officials were advised of the roundup plan, they notified the Germans that Danish Jews would now be permitted to enter Sweden. But by that time, the Nazis wanted extermination of the Jews, not freedom for them.

The Jews who had gone into hiding were so terrified of what

Danes arrested by the Germans on their way to prison.

was going to happen that initially there were some suicides, including a few who took poison capsules they had earlier requested from their physicians. The suicides stopped when the word spread that friends and neighbors were willing to help. Suddenly, there was hope.

When it became obvious that the majority of Jews were not to be found, the Nazis tried a new tactic. They offered to release all captured Danish soldiers and then an army general and a naval vice-admiral in exchange for information leading to the hiding places of Jews. The officers had been interned when the Germans declared the state of emergency on August 29, 1943. The Germans suspected the offer would be refused and it was. Another offer was made to release lower-ranking officers and lift the emergency restrictions which had been imposed, again in return for information. A few soldiers accepted this offer of release but with the rare exception of an informer, no details concerning the whereabouts of Jews were given in return.

Support for helping the Jews came from top Danish leaders as well. Former Danish Minister of Trade, Christmas Moeller, who had escaped to England in 1942, wrote an editorial that appeared in the underground newspaper, *Frit Danmark:* "We have helped the Jews and we shall go on helping them by all means at our disposal. If we desert them in their hour of misery, we desert our native country."

The leadership of the Danish state church, which was Lutheran, also protested the persecution of their fellow Jewish citizens. A statement was sent to Nazi leaders on September 29, 1943, and it was read from the pulpits in Danish churches the following Sunday. Signed on behalf of all the Danish bishops by H. Fuglsang Damgaard, Bishop of Copenhagen, it stated:

> *Wherever Jews are persecuted because of their religion or race it is the duty of the Christian Church to protest against such persecution, because it is in conflict with the sense of justice inherent in the Danish people and inseparable from our Danish Christian culture through centuries. True to this spirit and according to the text of the Act of the Con-*

50

*stitution all Danish citizens enjoy equal rights and re-
sponsibilities before the Law and full religious freedom.
We understand religious freedom as the right to exercise
our worship of God as our vocation and conscience bid us
and in such a manner that race and religion per se can
never justify that a person be deprived of his rights, freedom or property. Our different religious views notwith-
standing, we shall fight for the cause that our Jewish brothers and sisters may preserve the same freedom which we
ourselves evaluate more highly than life itself. With the
leaders of the Danish Church there is a clear understanding of our duty to be law-abiding citizens who will not
groundlessly rebel against the authorities, but at the same
time our conscience bids us to assert the Law and protest
against any violation of the Law. We shall therefore in
any given event unequivocally adhere to the concept that
we must obey God before we obey man.*

Another strong statement of support came from Pastor Ivor
Lange, the influential pastor of Frederiksberg Church, who declared, "Those who remain silent or disapprove by merely shrug-
ging their shoulders are no better than Nazi accomplices... I tell
you that I would rather die with the Jews than live with the Nazis."
In homes and churches all over Denmark people prayed for the
safety of the Jews.

In later years, Danes would recall September 29, 1943, as the
last day they participated in the "mutual negotiation and cooperation pact" which had been agreed upon at the time of invasion and
occupation. From this date the resistance swelled.

Refugees hid in these small fishing sheds in Copenhagen's Nordhavn (North Harbor) as they awaited boats that would carry them to safety in Sweden.

9

Planning the Exodus

Although most of the Jews had escaped the roundup and were in hiding, they obviously could not be kept hidden for very long. Where to go and what to do next? Sweden, across the water, presented the only escape route.

Sweden had been very careful to *appear* neutral during World War II. In reality, the country had cooperated with the Germans in various ways, such as shipping badly needed iron ore and ball bearings to Germany. Sweden also had allowed the use of her railways to transport German military personnel and materiel to their garrisons in occupied Norway. Furthermore, it was no secret that many Swedes were pro-German, including some members of the royal family as well as high ranking government officials and military officers.

In spite of this, just before the roundup became official, the Swedes had made two offers to the Germans involving the Danish Jews. The first offer was to put the Jews into a camp in Sweden "until the end of the war." The second was to allow Sweden to accept Danish children who were Jewish. Both offers were refused.

Once the roundup was ordered, the big question was whether Sweden would accept thousands of refugees, knowing that act would antagonize the Germans. Two factors helped the Swedish government arrive at a positive decision which would result in the saving of Denmark's Jews. The time was September, 1943, and the Germans were losing on the Russian front. The Swedes had no desire to be on the losing side when the war was over. Also, during that month of September, the Danish underground had smuggled Niels Bohr, the Danish physicist who was later to win the Nobel Prize, across the Sound to safety in Sweden. The Allies were anxious to have Bohr go to America to work on the atom bomb project.

Bohr suspected a roundup was going to take place and refused to leave Sweden until he was personally assured by King Gustav V that Jewish refugees from Denmark would be given sanctuary. Even after receiving Gustav's promise on the matter, Bohr refused to leave the country until he knew those in hiding were aware they had a place to go. When the information that Sweden would accept the Jews was broadcast over the radio and printed on the front pages of Swedish newspapers, Bohr finally left for London and then the United States.

Now the real work began in getting the Jews out of Denmark. Their hiding places were widely scattered so it was not easy to find all the refugees. But friends, neighbors, resistance groups and the underground quickly spread the news--Sweden offered a sanctuary for every Jew who could get there!

All of Denmark seemed ready to offer aid. Pastors urged their congregations to give sanctuary, and teachers helped students find shelter. The staffs of Copenhagen's hospitals organized their own rescue efforts and physicians gathered at a meeting and let it be known that Jews should turn to the hospitals for help. Two hundred young athletes, cross-country runners who were members of the Academic Rifle Club, spread throughout the forests, searching for refugees and encouraging them to make their way to the hospitals. Dr. Jørgen Kieler, Dr. Karl Henry Køster and others assuaged their loathing of the occupiers by converting Bispebjerg and other hospitals into way stations, hiding Jews in the psychiatric wing, the morgue, the attic, or putting them to bed as patients with good Danish names like Jensen, Petersen and Hansen. When a nurse asked a doctor what she should record on a new patient's chart, the doctor replied, "Just say he has German measles."

After the news of the planned roundup was made known, the efforts to get the Jews to safety involved an entire cross-section of Danes--friends and neighbors who hid them, police who looked the other way, religious leaders who allowed their churches to be used for sanctuary, doctors who hid them in their hospitals, newsmen, restaurant owners and fishing boat skippers. By car, taxi, streetcar, ambulance and railway, the Jews made their way to the coast. The Germans had allowed commercial vessels and boats of the fishing fleet to remain in the water ways, and the refugees and rescuers knew these boats were the only means to get to safety.

Fear pervaded the air. Jews were afraid of being caught and Danes feared they would be severely punished for helping Jews escape. Yet there was excitement, too, at this concerted major opportunity to defy the hated enemy. People in every walk of life wanted to protect the lives of their neighbors. All were part of the human wall of silence and brave network of conspiracy against the enemy.

At the southern end of the Sound there are fifteen miles of open water between Copenhagen and the Swedish city of Malmö, while in the north the Sound narrows to two miles at the point where it separates Denmark's Helsingør (Elsinore) from Sweden's Helsingborg. Hundreds of fishing boats and larger vessels were ready to take off with human cargo from Copenhagen's Nordhavn (North Harbor), Kalkbraenderihavnen (Limekiln Harbor), Tuborg and Kastrup Harbors and from almost every small harbor along the east coast of Zealand (Sjaelland), Denmark's largest island. Skippers helped each other with advice and information concerning the best departure places.

Local villagers, whose simple life rarely extended beyond the confines of their fishing villages, were not only eager to be a part of the resistance to the Nazis, but they also wanted to share kinship in their fellow Danes' heroic rescue mission. The small towns of Gilleleje, Snekkersten, Dragør and Stevns, the safest portals across the Sound to safety in various Swedish harbors, were soon filled with refugees. The Jews were offered housing in modest private homes and in apartments, hotels, inns and even garages. Hundreds, then thousands of refugees crowded into the little towns. No one was refused a place to stay.

The next step was to arrange with fishing boat skippers and captains of larger ships to take on the dangerous journey across the Øresund. There were many ready and willing to do that--sometimes for a price. This was unfair to those who could not pay, and though the Fisherman's Association negotiated with the skippers to agree to a uniform fee of $60 per passenger, no refugee was ever turned down for lack of money.

Sometimes German patrol boats forced a delay and refugees had to be hidden and fed for two or three days in wooden shacks and warehouses along the docks. Like so many others involved in the escape plan, fishermen were taking a great risk by sheltering and transporting Jews, but each Dane who helped became a link in the human chain of daring and secrecy that forged the historic rescue operation.

Some individuals and groups concentrated on smuggling Jews aboard established ferries going to Sweden or to the Baltic island of Bornholm, with the ferries often changing their course to discharge the refugees along the Swedish coast or to a Swedish naval patrol boat. On occasion even schooners, normally used to haul enormous boulders from the bottom of the sea, would take from thirty to one hundred persons aboard and deliver them safely. Around Helsingør (Elsinore) brave rescuers successfully used pilot boats, motorboats or the boats used in maintaining buoys and lights. Big or small, capable of carrying many or few, the immediate need was to use every boat to save the Jews.

It was at this point that Knud Dyby, yachtsman, policeman and resistance helper, was contacted to help make arrangements to get the Jacobsens, a Jewish family, across the Sound on one of the small boats of the fishing fleet. The ominous threat of the concentration camps dictated extreme urgency.

10

Concentration Camps

Word of the existence of the concentration camps began to spread in the early 1940s, and the specter of the camps haunted the Jews of Europe. Those prisoners who were fortunate enough to be released early on and the few who bribed their way or managed to escape in some other manner brought back tales too horrifying to be believed. But as evidence mounted, it became apparent these were, indeed, tales based upon fact.

The establishment of the camps was an outgrowth of policies instituted by Adolf Hitler, leader of the National Socialist German Workers Party (Nazis), when he was named Chancellor of Germany on January 30, 1933. In an effort to strengthen nationalist spirit Hitler began to implement policies aimed at ridding the country of "undesirables," especially Jews. At first the Jews were *invited* to leave their homeland, but they were well-established and highly regarded and few elected to leave. Shortly thereafter they were *ordered* to leave, but found almost no country willing to accept them. They were trapped in what was to become the nightmare of the Holocaust.

Some camps had been established in Germany as early as 1937, two years before the "official" beginning of World War II. They were designated as "concentration camps," "labor camps," or "euthanasia centers," (frequently converted for that purpose from previous nursing homes, mental hospitals or prisons). All were part of Hitler's grand scheme, the "Final Solution," which would get rid of the Jews and purify his country.

As the German army conquered country after country, Jews in each of those occupied lands were subject to Hitler's anti-Semitic

57

doctrines. Terror spread as many more camps were established.

In every country ground under the Nazi heel in Western Europe, with the notable exception of Denmark, "roundups" conducted by the Nazis routinely dragged Jews from their homes, out of synagogues and off the streets to be deported to the camps.

Victims were packed like cattle into railroad box-cars with no food, no ventilation and no sanitary facilities. The long trainloads slowly made their way to camp sites where the Jews were told they were going to work in factories or in fields producing needed goods and food for the Fatherland; the prisoners were frightened but obediently followed orders of the heavily armed guards. The sign at the entrance to Auschwitz, one of the most notorious of all the camps, read, "Arbeit Macht Frei" ("Work Shall Set You Free").

Many were death camps, where the only purpose was to kill the prisoners, predominantly Jews. The first step in selection took place immediately upon arrival, with the able-bodied sent one way and the elderly, sick and children ordered in another direction. Those who managed to survive the first selection were then introduced to the beginning of the dehumanization process--being tattooed with a number and having their hair shorn. Thereafter, inmates were known only by their numbers; the shorn hair was used in a variety of ways, including making thread, rope and stuffing for mattresses. The death camps, Auschwitz-Birkenau, Treblinka, Belzec, Majdanek, Chelmno and Sobibor, centered mainly in Poland, were extermination centers, designed for the purpose of killing inmates.

Some sites were work camps where prisoners were forced to make goods for home consumption in Germany and for Hitler's war machine. Prisoners labored under such horrendous conditions that often being sent to one of the work camps was tantamount to a death sentence. Inmates lived in barren barracks with little protection against extremes of hot or cold weather. The daily ration of food was far below acknowledged minimum standards and medical aid was almost non-existent. The work (slave labor) camps were located primarily in Germany and Austria, with a few scattered through France, Belgium and The Netherlands.

There were as many as 10,000 separate camp sites where prisoners were kept; some were enormous camps like Buchenwald, and others were temporary work places with just a few victims. Prisoners were subjected to every conceivable kind of abuse, including starvation, torture and inhumane medical experiments. Untold thousands died of suffocation when they were herded into "showers," where fatal Zyklon B gas spewed out of the shower heads instead of water. Crematoria were set up to burn the bodies of the dead and when that process proved too slow, victims were forced to dig their own mass graves before being shot.

It is estimated that four million Jews died in the slave-labor and death camps. Another two million died in ghettos, on death marches, and in massacres.

Millions of non-Jews also lost their lives. Hitler set out to eliminate those who did not conform to his idea of Aryan supremacy or who opposed his dictatorial philosophy. Included in his agenda of those to be exterminated, besides Jews, were the physically and mentally handicapped, homosexuals, Communists, Jehovah's Witnesses, and a variety of other asocials or "undesirables" as defined by the Nazis. The Gypsy population, those nomads who wandered the countryside singing and dancing and telling fortunes, were concentrated in Hungary and were nearly annihilated under Hitler's Aryan policy. Those who sympathized with the plight of the Jews, including some church leaders, were punished by being sent to concentration camps themselves. Also routinely arrested and sent to camps were those who opposed the regime by working for resistance and underground movements which had sprung up in occupied countries.

Almost from the beginning there had been rumors about the existence of the concentration camps, but in occupied countries only those people involved in anti-German activities evidenced any concern. Others either cooperated with authorities by revealing the location of Jews or ignored the issue. Even townspeople living in close proximity to the camps, such as Auschwitz, pretended the camps were not there and after the war claimed not to have known of their existence.

Thousands of Danes, including resistance workers and members of the police force, endured intense suffering in concentration camps (as well as in many German-run prisons within Denmark.) Their memories and experiences have not been forgotten.

The rest of the world did not know--or chose to ignore--mounting evidence of Hitler's fanaticism. It was with the Allied victory and the liberation of the camps that the true extent of the genocide was exposed. General of the Armies Dwight Eisenhower, who visited Ohrdruf, the first camp to be liberated, April 12, 1945, only at the insistent urging of his Jewish aide, Lt. Col. Lewis Weinstein, was horrified and outraged by the scenes he encountered. He ordered military photographers to take pictures, as proof of what he was seeing, and urged journalists and lawmakers to visit the camp immediately to bear witness. General Omar Bradley was so shocked he could not speak, and General George Patton, known for his bully-strength, disappeared behind a barracks and threw up. More than half a century later, Nazi concentration camps remain etched in the mind as one of the most frightening examples of inhumanity.

Theresienstadt

One apparent exception to the "usual" horrors of the camps was Theresienstadt, also known as Terezin. Originally a small town in Czechoslovakia, the 7,000 local non-Jewish residents had been expelled in May 1942. The entire town was transformed into a concentration camp and that was where the 464 Jews unable to escape the Danish roundup were sent. They were added to the 60,000 prisoners already living there in horribly overcrowded conditions. For the first time, Danish Jews were forced to wear the Star of David.

Many German Jews sent to Theresienstadt did not know what was in store for them. Some paid for what they thought was the privilege of going there, arriving elegantly dressed and even asking for "a room with a southern exposure." It did not take long for them to face the harsh reality of life in a concentration camp.

Whenever Theresienstadt reached its capacity the Nazis made regular "selections" and "selected prisoners" were sent to the Auschwitz death camp. But the Danish government kept such vigilant pressure on the Germans, constantly inquiring about Danish prisoners, that as a result no Danish Jews were ever selected for Auschwitz. Thanks also to this vigilance, Danish prisoners were allowed to receive Red Cross parcels from home which provided a precious supplement to their meager diets. The extra food was shared with other prisoners and helped many survive. Most Red Cross parcels in other camps were confiscated by the captors.

The Germans claimed that Theresienstadt was a typical camp and after lengthy and involved negotiations in Denmark, gave permission to allow a Red Cross delegation to inspect the site. To get ready for the unusual visit an increased number of prisoners were removed from the camp and sent to Auschwitz, so the place would look less crowded. A thorough clean-up and beautification was ordered. Jewish inmates white-washed houses, a library was established and a bandstand built in the town square. Dummy stores were set up, and a cafe, bank and school were erected. Gardens were planted. Some of the houses were painted on the inside and outfitted with furnishings, including pictures and potted plants. Danish Jews were installed in the lovely houses, with only two or three to a room.

No prisoners were allowed to speak to the visitors and the Red Cross delegates apparently were satisfied with the appearance of the camp. They watched children at play, saw inmates harvesting food in their vegetable gardens, and enjoyed music played on the bandstand by prisoners. The report the delegates submitted suggested no need for any changes. It is hard to believe they were so easily fooled. After the visitors left, Danish prisoners were the only ones allowed to remain in the refurbished houses.

Of the 144,000 Jews sent to Theresienstadt, only 19,000 survived. Of the 464 Danish Jews in the camp, 51 died and 425 (including some babies who were born there) survived.

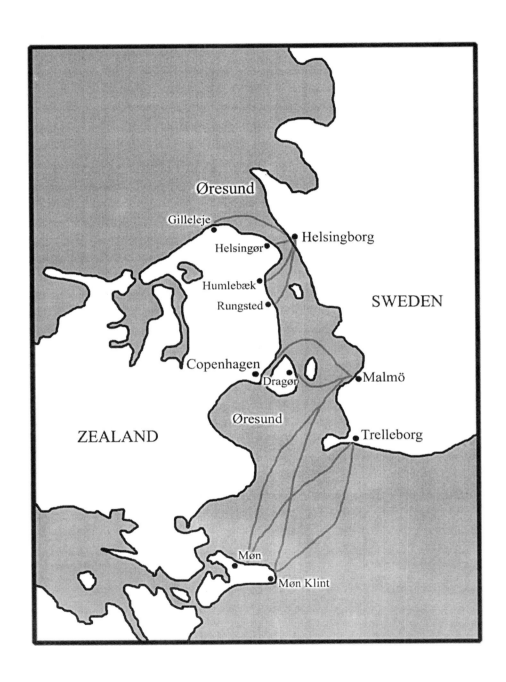

Escape Routes to Sweden

11

Boats in the Night

Even before the roundup of the Jews was ordered, Knud Dyby had helped make arrangements for a number of Danes to escape to Sweden. They were saboteurs who had an imperative need to leave the country because they were on the Nazis' most-wanted list. As a young man Dyby had enjoyed helping a friend haul his boat up into the Borghegn Wharf at the Kalkbraenderihavnen (Limekiln Harbor) dock, working to scrape, paint and outfit the boat in readiness for summer sailing. The connections he made, befriending the wharf owner and helping some of the fishing skippers prepare their boats, proved of great value at a later time when he was looking for a way to help those who needed to quickly leave the country. Making good use of these contacts with local fishermen, Dyby persuaded some of his skipper friends to use their boats to take saboteurs across the Sound to Sweden.

In the earlier mission, to get the time off he needed to help arrange the saboteurs' escape, Dyby told his boss, the police commissioner, that his grandmother had died. Now, October 1, 1943, the night of the roundup, a colleague asked for help in getting a Jewish neighbor out of Denmark. Dyby was not surprised at the request. His eyes light up as he recalls the conversation with the police commissioner: "Please, commissioner, my grandmother died *again* and I need to take a couple of hours off." The commissioner of course knew about the rescue work going on and replied, "Don't you think your grandmother would appreciate it if you used a police car?" Dyby said he did not think it was a good idea but thanked him for the offer anyway.

That evening Dyby met with his colleague, Frej, at the local chocolate shop. Frej had brought not only his neighbor, Valdemar Jacobsen, but also Jacobsen's wife and children and several other Jewish friends with their children as well. They were dressed in as many layers of warm clothing as they could pile on and were surrounded by boxes and suitcases. "I knew the Gestapo would easily spot them and figure out that they were trying to escape," says Dyby. So the Jacobsen group was divided into smaller groups and each was led by a "contact" man Dyby knew from his work in the resistance. They rode public buses and streetcars until they all met at a given location where cooperative and courageous taxi drivers took them to their destination, a point near the Limekiln Harbor in Copenhagen.

Dyby and his fisherman friend, Bernhard Ingemann-Andersen, otherwise known as Aage, negotiated the fare for "his" Jews with the fishing boat skippers. When the negotiations were completed, the Jacobsen family entourage were all hidden in the boats and sent on their way to safety. They were the first of the Jews Knud Dyby helped save.

For the next three weeks he was very busy making arrangements between two groups--those who frantically wanted to get out of Denmark and the fishermen who were willing to help. It was mostly by word of mouth that desperate Jews learned about the help that was being offered by Knud Dyby and others like him. "Somebody always seemed to know somebody in the chain of helpers. Word passed from one to another, from Jew to non-Jew; sometimes messages were even left at the police station with certain police officers who were known to be friendly to the refugees. Then, in the same way, we would send the word back about the details of time and place and so on."

Dyby negotiated with the skippers to keep the cost low and most were paid only enough to take care of their fuel and other expenses. "The fishermen were a motley bunch, but they were good people. Aage was a poor fisherman with a small half-open boat, always helpful and daring and sometimes he would even borrow bigger boats when he worked for us. He was a rather small and slender fellow, not too well kept or dressed but with a good sense of humor. I would make contact with him by phone, in guarded terms, of course, and then we'd meet at some inn where we could get a schnapps or a couple of sweet martinis to back up our courage."

Dyby remembers many others--Ellingsen, Larsen, Thomsen, Michaelsen and the Knudsen brothers. "In the beginning, it was individual 'pimpernels' who took upon themselves with a few friends to locate the refugees and find boats to transport them to safety. They did it not only as humanitarians but also as a way to resist the hated enemy."

One rescue is imprinted firmly in Dyby's memory. Just a few days after the beginning of the roundup, he received a telephone call from a girlfriend inviting him to dinner. "She said there was something urgent to talk about, and I knew from the sound of her voice that it was important." Arriving for dinner, Knud found not only his girlfriend but he also was introduced to her sister and the sister's boyfriend, 2nd Lieutenant Kalchar. Lt. Kalchar was an officer in the Danish army and admitted to being very nervous because he was Jewish on his father's side and had learned the Germans were inquiring at his home about his whereabouts. Dyby promised to see what he could do to help the young officer leave the country.

> *The next day I met my fishing/skipper friend, Aage, at Nordhavn Harbor and with only a little persuasion he agreed to take Kalchar to Sweden on his boat--as a 'free guest' with no money involved. Aage asked me to come along on the ride because his usual helper was sick. I agreed and called Kalchar and told him to meet me the next evening at the "S-Train," a railroad station.*

> *Then I realized I had a little problem. All the fishing skippers I knew were fairly short of stature, rugged in appearance, with wind-cracked skin darkened by the out-doors and faces always in need of a shave. Worn-down fingernails on big red hands were a trademark of their*

calling. I, on the other hand, was tall, blonde, blue-eyed, clean-shaven and pink-faced, with well manicured nails.

I didn't shave for 24 hours, then donned heavy black pants, a turtle-neck sweater, skipper hat and rubber boots. In spite of my "disguise" Kalchar did not have any trouble recognizing me when we met at the railroad station for the trip to the harbor.

With German navy personnel all around, Kalchar had to be smuggled onto the boat, even in the darkness of a typical miserable cold Danish night. Along with his little package of personal belongings, he was squeezed into the fishing boat's small cabin, already filled with nets, fishing tackle, tools, dried-out seaweed, worms and dead fish. The door to the cabin was locked with a great hanging lock and Aage said that if we were boarded he would just say he couldn't find the key.

Next, Aage had to deal with the harbor control. He went ashore to the Danish Police control with my "pass" and his dark green "Seaman's Sailing Permit" booklet. Because some of the police might have known me, I stayed on the boat and Aage told them I was too busy to be there myself. The permits were to be shown, if asked for, to the German police on shore as well as on their patrol boats.

In the night, with no running lights and hardly any harbor marking lights, we headed out. I stood next to Aage in his half-open cockpit, on a couple of rough boards almost on top of the diesel motor. Everything was in poor condition, including the motor and the quality of the fuel, but Aage had a fantastic sense of humor, he was adventuresome and daring and his enthusiasm seemed to override the faulty equipment and the old wooden boat.
If the German patrol saw us, they did not interfere. The

waves were on the rough side and I was drenched in the old and worn oil-skin coat, which might have fit Aage's helper, but definitely not me. I had the wheel while Aage was busy with some rope and fish hooks. We set the course on an old, cheap compass, and Aage promised we might be able to land in Borstarhusen in the morning.

In the early morning we could see Hveen Island and we also saw a couple of Swedish patrol boats but they did not bother our very small and slow boat. In the gray morning light we knew we were in Swedish territory and our passenger could feel free and safe. I do not think he had the feeling of any great freedom--he was dirty, wet, cold and I think he said he wanted to die. We convinced him to drink some terrible coffee from a thermos, while Aage had a beer. I was happy swallowing the water running down my face.

We tied up inside the long granite pier in Borstarhusen. There was plenty of docking space as most of the yachts and smaller boats had been hauled out of the water. We were welcomed by customs and police and the latter took Kalchar (or what was left of him) to the police station for a friendly interrogation. We were allowed to buy five gallons of fuel oil, a pack of pipe tobacco and some chocolate and then we were on our way back to occupied Denmark.

Aage did some fishing and managed to add to the supply of fish already in the so-called 'well-box,' some of them old enough, so Aage said, that they recognized him. Fishing was something I was never interested in.

With daytime drawing near and with me at the wheel most of the time, we soon were in Danish territorial waters. Although I was dressed as a fisherman, and miserably wet, unshaven and uncombed, I was more nervous

*than I had ever been. I felt absolutely stupid and I was
sure that if we were boarded the Germans would laugh
themselves silly with me claiming to be a fisherman. I
knew I would end up with the Gestapo who would inter-
rogate me and in time find that I was a police officer and
involved in some resistance activities.*

*I promised myself that I would not be a fisherman again
but would let the skippers, who knew their business and
boats, take care of that end of the job, while from my home
and from the police station I could help Jews and saboteurs get to the boats and larger ships for transportation
to freedom.*

As word of the roundup of the Jews became known, more
groups of rescuers were formed by such leaders as Robert Jensen,
Gyberg, Kiaer, Sejr, and many others, who used freighters and
ferry boats, together with smaller boats, to transport hundreds of
refugees. An organization called *Speditoren* (Freight Forwarder)
probably did more than any other to use bigger ships in the rescue
effort. Leaders of this group were so secretive that even today it is
almost impossible to know the exact extent of their efforts. In
October 1943, two radio wholesalers, Gyberg and Robert Jensen,
"shipped out" hundreds of refugees from various parts of the
Zealand coast. Shortly thereafter, Gyberg and Jensen attended a
meeting in Stockholm, together with other important Danish rescuers and resisters, where they discussed not only the refugee
work that was being done but also the concern involving financing of their resistance enterprises.

Leif B. Hendil, a Danish journalist who had fled to Sweden
before October 1943, and later known by the code name "Hot,"
was delegated to establish an organization which would encom-
pass the various resistance groups. Hendil had been the well-
known editor of a Copenhagen newspaper, *Ekstrabladet*, whose
anti-German sentiments and work with the underground had
angered the Germans. Because of his connections with people of
importance in both countries he was able to secure financing for

the organization, to be known as the DSRS, the Danish-Swedish Refugee Service. Its members were Danes who already had made their escape to Sweden. Included in the group were Danish saboteurs, politicians and newsmen who were on German lists to be arrested.

Hendil, in a conference with Swedish Foreign Minister Gunther, offered to have the DSRS provide everything necessary for a secret courier service between the two countries, including finances, boats and equipment, with Sweden only providing gasoline. Gunther agreed, and the DSRS was on its way. The Swedes eventually helped in the forging of secret documents, providing protection from the Gestapo, and Swedish patrols that "looked the other way" on the coast.

The DSRS purchased about a dozen boats, and at night these would meet the boats of the Danish underground between the territorial boundaries of the two countries. Passengers were picked up and mail exchanged, which helped reduce the risk of Danish boats being reported back to the Germans. During the roundup the DSRS joined the effort to rescue Jews, transferring anxious refugees from one boat to another and taking them to the Refugee Service's own safe harbor in Sweden (see page 76).

Dyby remembers, "We were careful not to have refugees and anyone on the Gestapo's most-wanted list on the same boat. If a saboteur had been caught and interrogated by the Nazis he could have been made to give information that led to others and that might well have endangered the chain of contacts for the whole organization."

There were many groups trying to get onto the fishing boats and the frightened, cold refugees huddled together in the small wooden fishing sheds where the fishermen kept their tools and nets. They were old and young, men and women, trembling children, bearded rabbis, all pale and distressed as they faced an uncertain future. An eerie silence settled over the harbor, with parents quieting children for fear of alerting German patrols. The danger was sometimes so intense that doctors drugged smaller children and babies to ensure they would not imperil the refugees or their rescuers.

Swedish authorities in Malmö allowed the Danish-Swedish Refugee Service their own dock in the Malmö Harbor.

Assisting the Jews became a turning point for many active resisters and for much of the Danish population in general. "We can do it" became the motto, and cooperation cemented the growing resistance groups into a cohesive unit wherein they all worked together.

In the harbor towns Jews huddled on shore, waiting for pre-arranged lights to appear in the darkness. When the lights could finally be seen, the refugees sometimes scrambled a hundred yards through ice-cold water three or four feet deep, gratefully grasping outstretched hands as they were hauled into the boats.

The fishing boats with their "passengers" took off from many of the little harbors along the Danish coast. Friendly Danes served as scouts at harbor entrances and sent back warnings whenever a Gestapo unit or patrol boat was nearby. Even though German navy personnel were thinly spread out on Denmark's long coast, those concerned with the rescue operation were thankful for the typical stormy fall weather that combined with dark nights to make the rescue effort successful. "We made sure every boat had a full load of refugees, even if they didn't have money to pay. No Jewish person was turned away because he didn't have money."

Some of Knud's fellow officers on the police force spent their time on duty serving as telephone operators at the station. When he appeared, these cooperative colleagues handed him the list of calls which had not been transferred through the normal channel to the police sergeant's desk. Some of the calls were from Knud's girlfriends, but many were from people he scarcely knew, requesting a meeting as soon as possible. "Instinctively I knew what they wanted and so would meet them at their homes." Almost always the meetings involved pleas to help make arrangements for Jews or saboteurs who desperately wanted to get to Sweden--someone known to a friend or neighbor or to the callers themselves.

After helping to make the rescue arrangements for the Jacobsen family, Dyby rarely learned the names of the people he was helping. He says, "I purposely did not write down any names. I tried not to remember any names if I heard them. It was a risk to know something, and I did not want to know anything more than I had to know, in case I was caught by the Gestapo and they questioned me. Even though I loved to sail, I did not go on too many of the trips myself because I already knew too much."

It did not require much police work on Knud's part to determine that the requests were legitimate and a boat trip was absolutely necessary. Often, over a cup of "ersatz" coffee, names and meeting places were arranged. Because Knud's skipper contacts were frequently booked a day or two ahead, the refugees had a brief chance to make their last-minute arrangements, even if they could not stay in their own homes during that time.

Shortly after making arrangements at one such meeting Knud met three middle-aged men in his neighborhood. Making believe they were old friends, they paired off and entered a streetcar from two different ends. The streetcar, like all cars and trucks and other means of transportation, whether Danish or German, was dimmed so it could not be seen from the air. Only an inch of blue light was permitted on the front and rear and interior of autos and streetcars. Although streetcars generally were crowded with people during the day, by nighttime there were very few on board, and once curfew hour started only city workers, policemen, doctors and nurses were allowed to travel. In the dusky interior of the streetcar, all went well for the first part of the journey. Knud remembers what happened next:

> *We had to change streetcars for the next part of our trip to the harbor front. That was when we had a scare. We were practically alone on a street corner, close to the National Museum, and we saw a patrol of Germans coming our way. It was possible the patrol would demand to see our identification, as any gathering roused suspicion.*
>
> *We hoped we had seen them before they saw us. We knew we could not run, but fortunately the street we were on was being repaired and we saw a long, deep excavation, marked with the familiar inch-long blue lights to warn passing pedestrians.*
>
> *The four of us jumped into the excavation, the three of*

them with small packages under their arms and myself with a drawn pistol. We silently squeezed ourselves into as small a space as possible and covered our faces. We heard the Germans talking and the sound of their boots marching past our hiding place. I think I would have used my pistol to defend us, but fortunately it did not become necessary. We all knew that for every German soldier shot, some Danes might have been executed in retaliation.

I was very happy when I finally saw my "friends" take off on the boat!

One of the fishing boat skippers Dyby regularly used was caught by the Germans and had to endure painful and brutal questioning. Dyby knew if any more of "his" fishermen were caught there would be more beatings because the Gestapo wanted to know who gave the skippers their orders and how they made contact with the refugees. Dyby set up a small apartment filled with information that was up-to-date but not very important. Nobody lived in the apartment. If a skipper was caught he would hold out under the interrogation as long as he could and then tearfully "reveal" the apartment's location. The fake apartment could only be used one time but it was easy to change from place to place.

At one point the Gestapo used trained German shepherd dogs to sniff out passengers hidden under the floorboards. Once again, ingenuity outsmarted the oppressors. Dyby explains, "We fooled them. We had a pharmaceutical laboratory concoct a special powder made of a mixture of human blood plasma and cocaine. The blood attracted the dogs and when they sniffed the powder they couldn't smell anything at all. After that, the powder was sprinkled on the gangplanks of all the boats and we didn't have any more trouble with the dogs finding our passengers."

In only a few weeks the rescue of the Jews was completed. There had been more than 700 crossings of the Sound. Some had been made in large ships and ferries which could take dozens of refugees at a time, but many of those taking flight made the journey hidden in cramped, smelly quarters of small fishing boats that had space for only a few each crossing. The alternative was a different journey, leading to a concentration camp. Everyone knew that.

12

Safely in Sweden

Jewish refugees, arriving in Sweden by the hundreds, frequently were piqued when required to appear at a Swedish office for in-depth interrogations. Uprooted, tired and stressed, they had anticipated being greeted with open arms, not with intense questioning. The Swedes, constantly on the alert to protect themselves and their neutrality, strengthened their police, customs and coast guard.

But once the questions were over, every effort was made to make the newcomers welcome. In 1943, Danes in the Danish Embassy and consulate offices in Sweden formed committees to help the refugees and soon others formed a *Modtager og Hjaelpe Komite* (Receiving and Helping Committee). Banks in Helsingborg and Malmö made special arrangements so the new arrivals could change their money--although many came only with the clothes they were wearing.

Refugee committees, with the help of the Swedish Red Cross, the Save The Children organization and the police, first provided shelter by filling all available hotels and *pensions* with Danes. Later, schools and meeting halls were used, and the committee provided food, beds, sleeping bags and toilet articles for all who needed help.

The Danish Embassy made up specific refugee passports, and in a short while the refugee office, in an agreement with various labor unions in Sweden, arranged for all willing hands to be given some kind of job, although not always in the same trade or occupation previously held in Denmark. Many able-bodied men were sent to work in Swedish forests, and women worked as cooks.

Who, When, and How Many
Did the Danish-Swedish Refugee Service Rescue?

Between October 1943 and May 5, 1945,
1888 individuals were transported to Sweden.

Number:	
October - 1943	41
November	152
December	320
January - 1944	107
February	87
March	123
April	143
May	90
June	106
July	88
August	60
September	35
October	86
November	23
December	33
January - 1945	22
February	33
March	121
April	139
May	79

Occupations:	
Tradesmen	273
Industrial Workers	181
Students	131
Office Workers	110
Military Personal	65
Police	58
Artists	37
Sailors/Fishermen	33
Engineers	30
Editors/Journalists	25
Teachers	21
Architects/Draftsmen	20
Doctors	20
Farmers	16
Politicians	13
Housing Supervisors	11
Nurses	10
Lawyers	7
Pastors	3
Sales Representatives	3
Diverse Others	87
Children or Unknown	726

Nationalities:

Danish	1756	Dutch	8	Austrian	2
German	46	Polish	7	Icelandic	2
American	23	French	6	Italians	2
British	12	Czech	4	Russians	1
Norwegian	11	Belgium	3	Stateless	2
		Swedish	3		

The elderly and those who could not find jobs received a subsistence stipend along with financial help for apartments, clothing and medical care, with many Danish doctors in Sweden donating much of their time to caring for refugees without pay. The social system in Sweden was at the time a good one, and the Swedes were generous in offering their services in hospitals or wherever refugees needed medical assistance.

Even though Malmö was the town closest to Copenhagen, Danes were advised not to settle there, and instead, many established themselves in the university town of Lund and others in the lovely town of Gothenburg. Wherever there were enough children, schools for Danish children were started and the DSRS boats brought school books across the Sound to Sweden for the youngsters. High school and university students were assisted in their studies at the Swedish academies of higher learning.

Jewish refugees with talents in fine art, architecture, and sculpture, found themselves warmly received, not only in the academies in Stockholm, but in the homes of Swedish artists, as well. Jews gathered in small groups to study their law and heritage with rabbis who, like themselves, were refugees.

Starting in late 1943, a *Dansk Pressetjeneste* (Danish Press Service) was established, with the purpose of keeping Danish refugees well informed. The editors strove conscientiously to "sift" the news from occupied Denmark so that the free world would be told the truth about what was happening in Denmark. The underground paper, *Information*, founded by Børge Outze, whom Knud helped flee from the Gestapo, was the paper most widely credited with presenting actual happenings of life as they occurred in Denmark. Another of Knud's very good friends, Svenn Seehusen (now deceased), was elected editor of the first monthly publication, *Danskeren* (The Dane), which later was issued weekly.

The many Danish police officers in Sweden successfully established their own Corps. Their training included the investigation of refugees who might be spies for the Germans or "quislings" planted by the Gestapo. The Corps also established a "swat" group ready to "take care" of Danish criminals returning from Germany, where they had been supported by the Nazis. Fortunately the

Corps saw very little action after the Germans surrendered, even though a few hardy Nazis engaged them in some gun fire.

Danish military and naval personnel in Sweden received permission to recruit Danes into a military unit called *Den Danske Brigade* (The Danish Brigade), whose purpose was to be prepared to fight Germans at whatever time the Brigade would be able to return to Denmark.

13

Civil Protection Service

In 1940 a Civil Protection Service (CPS) was established, composed of men who had exemptions from military service, frequently because of their status as students. They worked for the Service five days a week and served in a special department within the police force. Dyby remembers:

> *They were interesting young people and often would accompany the police on their rounds--one policeman and one CB (CPS) member. I remember they had dark blue uniforms made of heavy wool. They did not carry guns. We called them "føl" (Danish for colt) because the two of them together were like a mare and her colt.*

The young volunteers were high spirited and had to be supervised carefully because they often instigated some "interesting" but non-regulation activity. One time a lady telephoned the office in the middle of the night and said she thought it was terrible the way the young men in the CPS were being treated. "Look up at your watch tower. That man should not have to walk outside on that very narrow ledge." Of course, the young man should have been inside the tower, but was having some fun walking on the narrow ledge in the dark.

Another time, Dyby remembers, a caller to the CPS complained of noise coming from a nearby church. Usually two men were deployed to the church tower to be on the alert for possible bombing attacks. One quiet night at 2:00 a.m., a CPS worker whiled away the hours playing the church organ and became so enthusiastic the crescendos of his music could be heard blocks away, to the disturbance of the sleeping neighborhood.

As a policeman, Dyby had a group of young CPS workers under his guidance. They knew he liked a good party. Out in the district, blackout curtains blowing from an open window frequently indicated just such a party was taking place. More than once the CPS knocked on a door and warned those inside they were making too much noise. The party goers then invited the CPS volunteers to come inside for coffee or "something stronger." The CPS insisted on reporting the incident to their leader (Dyby) and under the guise of investigating what was going on, he too would stay for an hour or two enjoying the festivities--a pleasant respite from his more serious duties.

Since the fun-loving CPS members did not always follow the rules, it was up to Dyby to keep them in line, but he did not want to assume responsibility for all their actions. He divided the CPS into groups with a leader accountable for each group. The system worked well, and many problems were solved without Dyby being involved and having to report the matter to his superiors.

In 1944, after the Germans had arrested most of the police force and deported them to concentration camps, the Civil Protection Service remained active but without the authority of the police department. Helpful to the underground, they also assisted in the "Bernadotte Action" initiated by Count Folke Bernadotte, President of the Swedish Red Cross. This involved assisting refugees who, through negotiations by Count Bernadotte, had been released from concentration camps in Germany and were traveling across Denmark in order to reach Sweden. The CPS also frequently filed reports alerting authorities when it appeared, to quote Shakespeare, "something was rotten in the state of Denmark."

14

The General Strike

Hitler became increasingly impatient and angry with the defiance shown by the Danes and in June 1944, after several more acts of sabotage, the Nazis responded with reprisals which included the execution of eight Danish resisters. The cycle of retaliation gained momentum, resulting in the death of scores of Danish civilians. Many homes and businesses were destroyed. Angered by the reprisals and frustrated by a curfew, workers of Burmeister and Wain, the nation's largest shipbuilders, went on strike. Starting on Monday, June 26, 1944, work stopped on ships which were being built or repaired for the Germans.

The next day, Tuesday, the Germans issued a warning, with dire threats if strikers did not show up to work as usual. When the strike continued, the Nazis started a reign of terror that included firing at random into crowds in the streets and into Danish homes. Many Danish civilians were killed and many more injured by the notorious Schalburg Corps, Danes who earlier had volunteered to fight with the Germans against the Russians on the eastern front.

The average Danish citizen considered the Wehrmacht soldiers and members of the SS and the Gestapo a nuisance, but they vehemently hated the three groups composed of Nazi-oriented fellow Danes: one was the Schalburg Corps, another the Frikorps, (Danes wearing German uniforms and serving in the German army), and "HIPOS," the Hilf Polizei (Help Police), whose ranks included Danish criminals assisting the German police after the regular Danish police had been arrested.

Knud remembers that even his younger brother, Sven, age 20, was arrested at their home in Randers on June 3, 1944, and taken to Gestapo headquarters in Aarhus. Sven had been a member of an illegal Boy Scout group and when the scoutmaster was arrested for anti-German activities Sven's name was found on a list in the scoutmaster's possession. Although he had no information of any importance to the Germans, Sven was treated roughly at the prison. Knud advised his parents to keep constant pressure on the Germans and encouraged a letter-writing campaign which resulted in letters on Sven's behalf being sent by the mayor of Randers, the family pastor and the schoolmaster, German teacher Wassman, who also was a printing customer of Knud's father. At the urging of the boy's mother, Dagmar, Wassman went to the Gestapo headquarters and was able to arrange for the release of her son and another man who was being held as a prisoner. On June 21, 1944, Knud received a cable in Copenhagen: "Sven home again." Ironically, Wassman was later liquidated by the underground because he was suspected of working with the Germans as a "quisling."

On Friday, June 30, 1944, a week after the eight Danes were executed, the resisters called for an extension of the strike. The walkout and shutdown spread to other factories and businesses in Copenhagen. The Germans retaliated by cutting off water, gas and electricity. Roads to the capital city were blocked so that food supplies could not be brought in.

But the Germans again misjudged the strong will of the Danes. The general strike spread from town to town and city to city until the nation shut down. Neighbor helped neighbor and groups banded together to offer food and supplies to each other. Frustrated and furious, the Nazis could do little to stop the strike.

The Danes never lost their sense of humor. At the height of the strike the Germans put a couple of armored tanks in the center of the Town Hall Square in Copenhagen. Danes on their way to work the next morning laughed when they saw the sign a prankster had placed at the base of the tanks: "Saelges," (For Sale).

Finally, the Freedom Council, the secret organization of underground leaders, met with government representatives and urged that the Germans should be told the strikes were a protest against

A German soldier in full battle gear watches a Danish crowd on the streets of Copenhagen.

German restrictions. The Council wanted the Germans to enforce stricter control over the Schalburg Corps and to abolish martial law and the curfew. They also wanted the roads to Copenhagen re-opened and no reprisals for the strike. But negotiations reached a standstill and settlement did not appear possible.

Georg Duckwitz, who in 1943 had been responsible for alerting a trusted Danish politician of the impending roundup, now played a pivotal role in the strike negotiations. Because of his experience in the shipping industry he not only had excellent connections with Burmeister and Wain's management personnel, but also with the striking workers. Through his efforts the stalled bargaining resumed.

On July 3rd the Germans gave in. Workers reluctantly returned to their jobs, but their unity and determination had proved to be an effective weapon against the enemy and set a courageous example to workers in other occupied nations.

A variety of strikes by the Danes continued to plague the Germans, particularly in those industries obliged to work for the enemy. Sabotage became more daring with spectacular results. The German air base at Aalborg, a constant threat to the Allies, was completely destroyed by saboteurs. Acting on information supplied by the Danish Resistance, the RAF, with finite precision, bombed Gestapo headquarters at Aarhus, Odense, and Copenhagen, from low altitudes. Some arrested Danish resisters being held by the Nazis managed to escape in the confusion and many Germans were killed and numerous German records were destroyed. As the Allies approached Denmark in March 1945, the country's railroad system was put out of service completely. The resistance also pulled off another miracle: every tugboat in the country headed secretly to Sweden, rendering the Danish ports useless to the Germans.

15

Stories of the Resistance

The "General Strike" that began at the end of June 1944, reflected the growing frustrations of the Danish people with the German occupation. Knud Dyby too felt this frustration and continued his work in the resistance. In the summer of 1944, he formally joined the Danish-Swedish Refugee Service (DSRS) though he was still a member of the police force.

On September 19, 1944, Dyby's life changed dramatically. This was the day that the Nazis arrested the entire Danish police force, placing their own forces in direct control. Dyby narrowly escaped arrest since he was off-duty at the time. When he answered the call of the siren, he saw that the police station was surrounded by German soldiers, and so he went "underground," taking with him the sack of forms for passports, birth certificates, and identification cards. He was one of the lucky ones. He was also fortunate because he and other officers who escaped the Nazi net technically remained on the police force and continued to have their salaries paid by the government. Though he could no longer serve in an official capacity, Dyby knew he could continue to contribute in other ways.

The presence of the Gestapo and German soldiers was a constant reminder to Dyby and other helpers how dangerous their work was. German soldiers, usually in groups of three, wearing steel helmets and carrying loaded machine guns, patrolled the streets night and day. Surprise arrests by the Gestapo were almost always followed by brutal interrogations and sometimes killings. That was enough to keep resistance and underground workers and their helpers constantly on the alert.

By the middle of 1944, the underground was causing serious problems for the Germans. The Gestapo increased its efforts to find and imprison resistance workers and that slowed the work of the DSRS. Two couriers from the DSRS headquarters in Sweden arrived in Copenhagen to help reorganize the group. Leif Hendil was one of the men, though he went by the code name of "Hot"; the other man was called "Ras". Knowing that Dyby had contacts to get refugees to Sweden, Ras requested a meeting, after which they met several more times. "By that time I'd been successful in sending refugees and mail and other goods to Sweden and I was pretty cocky. I told Ras I would even send him elephants if that was what the DSRS wanted and had the money to pay for. I'm glad they didn't take me up on it, but I just wanted to let them know if they would support us, we could supply them with many things from Denmark."

The DSRS was minutely involved in many details and areas of the resistance. "We sent over some important people, like Arne Sørensen, who was a member of the Freedom Council and earlier had been Minister for Church Affairs in the Danish cabinet. Supposedly he had to go to Sweden on a 'study mission,' but actually he went there to contact Ebbe Munck, the most important contact man between politicians in Denmark and the Allies." Munck administered economic aid to the DSRS and other refugee organizations in Sweden, and he was the one who made the decision when Gestapo headquarters in Denmark were to be bombed or sabotaged.

Sometimes mail picked up in Copenhagen for delivery to Sweden contained secret information and/or large sums of money. Chris was a courier who picked up mail and brought it to Knud for transit. One evening while carrying a yellow envelope which was to be delivered to Knud, he was seen by a German patrol when he ran from one streetcar to board another at a transfer point. He backed against a darkened store and slipped the envelope down his back so that it came to rest standing against the wall. Stepping forward into the light he innocently responded to questions by the patrol. They let him go, but a shaken Chris reported the incident to Knud who sent him back to successfully retrieve the envelope that fortunately was still resting against the wall.

The DSRS also helped provide vital fuel for the fishing boats, gave financial help when needed and offered little gifts of chocolate and tobacco which were much appreciated, those items being rare luxuries in Denmark. The group also raised money to help Danish refugees get settled during their exile in Sweden.

Leif Hendil understood the need to meticulously maintain records, including data and logs on the numbers of people assisted, sailings, and all money spent (see page 76). This fact made the DSRS one of the most important refugee organizations and its accomplishments are listed in official Danish state archives.

The work of the resistance continued unabated until the end of the war and many heroic tales were written in blood. In October 1944, Robert Jensen (code name "Tom") met with four other resistance workers in a first floor apartment in Frederiksberg. The Gestapo had been tipped off and surrounded the building. When no one answered their knock, they broke down the door. "Tom" and "Torkild" (Svend Trondbjerg) tried to flee out the back door but were shot and killed. A third person, Algreen-Petersen, escaped out a window, but was wounded and captured on the sidewalk below. A fourth man by the name of Geisler, whom the British had earlier dropped by parachute, was caught, but he fought his captors in the street, jumped a high fence and escaped. Subsequently, Leif "Hot" Hendil warned members of the underground about a helper named "Søren." It had been discovered that "Søren" had accepted money from the Gestapo in return for revealing the address and time of the meeting in which "Tom" and "Torkild" were killed. A short time later, "Søren" was interrogated by members of the resistance, and after it became clear that he had lied, he confessed and was executed.

Not all actions were this brutal. Because Germans needed fish for food, Danish fishermen were allowed to continue going to sea. Sometimes, however, the skippers were so busy carrying material to Sweden they didn't have time to fish and had to buy a catch from the Swedes to have as proof they were doing what they were supposed to do!

Besides refugees, the fishing boats carried small packages and mail. Important mail, the kind that was helpful to the Allies or subversive to the Germans, had to be carefully hidden. For this, skippers used a variety of means--hollowed out masts, double walls, double bottoms and empty waterproof oil and gas containers. Heavy metal boxes attached to the outside of the boat under the water line made good hiding places that were hard for the enemy to detect.

From the latter part of 1944 until the end of the war in May 1945, "Dyby's boats" transported mail, news and intelligence information to Sweden three to four times a week, sometimes more. For this the skippers were paid 350 Kroner (about $70 at that time) to cover fuel and living expenses. If they carried a refugee, they would be paid 500 Kroner (about $100).

The story of a particular sack of mail remains clearly in Dyby's memory. One evening he and his friend, Sofie, rode their bicycles to the home of Larsen, who was to take the sack to the harbor. "It was always safer to ride with a lady because it looked like you were a romantic couple or going to a party." Dyby told Larsen the streets looked safe and offered to go with him to the harbor that evening, because the fishing boats usually took off between 5:00 and 6:00 a.m. Larsen declined, saying his nephew would help him in the morning, so Dyby and Sofie left. The next day, when Larsen and his nephew headed for the harbor at 5:00 a.m., a German patrol of three soldiers, guns in hand, came around the corner. Larsen and his nephew tried to hide in a doorway but were caught by the Nazis. "That was the only sack of mail we lost," sighs Dyby. The Germans were busy for a long time, looking into the information the mail provided. Larsen and his nephew were imprisoned and beaten, until the Gestapo was convinced they were only transporting the mail from one place to another. Larsen was sent to a concentration camp and his nephew was put into prison. Both survived.

A fisherman named Ellingsen was a very solid family man with a well-kept vessel. He made more trips than anyone else and was admired by "Hot" (Hendil) for his precision and honesty. Dyby's contact with the fishermen was either at the dock or some-

One day's "underground" mail sent to Sweden on a Danish-Swedish Refugee Service boat in 1944.

times by means of a telephone call to wherever they lived, but in order not to endanger them or their families he seldom visited them in their homes. Dyby did not know where Ellingsen lived. Then one night Dyby enjoyed an evening out with a lady friend from his home town. She later invited him up to her rented room. When the lady told Dyby that her landlord was a fishing skipper who had helped some of her Jewish friends escape to Sweden, Dyby looked at the sign on the door and saw that he had visited Ellingsen without his or Ellingsen's knowledge. Definitely not a good idea!

One resistance worker, a friend of Dyby's, was a man named Marx, a German Jew who had escaped to Sweden and served as a courier for the underground. He had a set of papers identifying him as a Swede. One night Marx and his companion, Staermose, were on a boat that was stopped by Germans patrolling the Sound. Because his so-called "Swedish" boat was not supposed to be in Danish territorial waters, Marx and Staermose claimed they were just Swedish fishermen whose boat had gone off course. Then Marx remembered that he also was carrying a Danish identification card for his forays into Denmark. He had to get rid of the card quickly, so getting permission to relieve himself over the side of the boat he ate his Danish identification card while performing this function. When he got back to Sweden, Marx joked that the identification card tasted good but he hated the flavor of his photograph!

In another incident, Dyby was meeting with a member of the underground Naval Intelligence. Because the Gestapo by now had an "unfriendly interest" in both men, the two had been careful to request window seats in the restaurant where they were meeting. In the course of the meal Dyby glanced outside and saw a long black car being parked at the curb. The driver was obviously Gestapo. Realizing they had been followed, they swallowed their drinks, "forgot" to wait for the bill and quickly disappeared through the kitchen, out the back door, over a wall and into the crowd on a nearby busy street.

Dyby remembers the time 144 fine Swiss watches were sent to Denmark on the boats. "It was great using them as timers for bombings and explosives." School supplies were sent to Sweden for Danish children living there, reports were exchanged and the underground newspaper, *Information,* was sent across the Sound. The paper was copied and distributed in Sweden and other occupied countries to make news of what was happening in Denmark available without German censorship. Several copies of each issue were sent by air to the Danish representative at the central organization of the Allies in London.

One group associated with the DSRS, called "1944," was led by a man named Ib. M. B. Christensen, code name "Knud"! At one point Knud Dyby received some pistols and ammunition which he was to share with the other Knud. "I got the address of their headquarters, and I must say, when I got close I got nervous because it was guarded by people with colored hair and wearing dirty raincoats. It would not take much for the Gestapo to see that they were looking at underground workers. I met their leader, Knud, and delivered the guns. One of that group's important actions had been to go in at night and destroy the files in the German Chamber of Commerce office in Copenhagen. Unfortunately, on a saboteur action in April 1945, just a few weeks before capitulation by the Germans, "Knud" (Christensen) was killed by the Gestapo."

Another remarkable piece of ingenuity was using the Germans' own aircraft to carry messages from the underground in Denmark to friendly Danish accomplices in Sweden. Before German planes took off from the Danish airport, resistance helpers stored the wheel-stop blocks inside the plane. The wheel-blocks, which had been hollowed out to hold messages, were picked up by sympathetic workers when the plane landed in Sweden. The Germans must have thought that putting wheel-blocks inside the plane was a very strange Danish custom because this was not done anywhere else.

Besides the planes, German trains crossing from Sweden to Norway were also used to help the resistance workers. Messages were hidden in a secret spot under the third railroad car. When the cars arrived in Sweden they carried not only German troops but also vital information which was retrieved by the underground.

Even ambulances were used to help the cause. Ambulance companies were privately owned so they were able to go about their business as usual. Because the Germans also used the ambulances in case of emergency, they ordinarily did not stop these vehicles for routine inspections. Friendly ambulance drivers often helped the underground by transporting refugees, saboteurs and ammunition. One time, when an ambulance was being used to move 200 rifles and hand grenades from one place to another, the driver was stopped by a German patrol and asked to explain where he was going. The driver offered to let the Germans check his ambulance, but he also mentioned, "We are on our way to a special clinic for contagious diseases with a person who has meningitis." The Germans quickly sent the ambulance on its way without an inspection.

One of Dyby's favorite stories is about a Danish yacht which General Pancke, an officer in the Gestapo, commandeered for his own use. The officer was pleased that the Danish captain of the yacht agreed to stay on and run the boat. General Pancke invited a group of high-ranking army and Gestapo officers to go on the first trip and the yacht docked in a small harbor north of Copenhagen where the group went ashore to an inn for lunch. When they returned, they discovered the yacht and its Danish captain had taken off for Sweden. For the remainder of the war the Danish-Swedish Refugee Service (DSRS) made good use of that yacht, meeting fishing boats and picking up Danish refugees and taking them to safety.

Dyby also remembers the time the British were doing some bombing raids on their own and that would delay his work for a while. "Once they bombed a factory where motors were being made. I lived only 100 meters from the factory. I was lucky I wasn't hurt!"

One of the members of the underground was a high-ranking employee of the Copenhagen telephone company, Mr. Orlamundt. He was the contact person between the underground and the phone service. Dyby says, "I met him two or three times every week. He had discovered that the Gestapo was listening in on conversations of suspected underground workers, so he would find out from phone company engineers which lines were being tapped. He and I would then get together and he would share with me which lines we had to be careful about." Unfortunately, with the help of informers the Germans were told of Orlamundt's activities and early in 1945 he was arrested. On the day of the arrest, Dyby received a phone call from another of his resistance contacts, Paul Jensen, who had been in touch with Orlamundt every day. "When I got that call I was able to warn our Swedish friends and workers in Copenhagen and told them to move their offices."

In the fall of 1944, Danish saboteurs bombed the Langebro Bridge, the drawbridge that linked the island of Amager to the city of Copenhagen. The damaged bridge would not go up or down, effectively stopping German ships. The Germans quickly repaired it in order to get harbor traffic back to normal, but the saboteurs again stopped traffic by strategically placing a bomb and sinking a ship. Once more, all traffic stopped until the ship was removed from the harbor.

Dyby even helped make the arrangements for some German army deserters to get out of Denmark. "I could understand why they were anxious to leave. They would have been in real trouble if the Germans had caught them." Several of these German soldiers were actually internationally known circus acrobats and at their departure they gave Dyby their uniforms, dog-tags and side arms, all of which could be used by the resisters. Dyby remembers that he left the uniforms in a suitcase stored at a graphic machinery company whose owner had been kind enough to give him free rent and storage room for his work in photoengraving patents. But within a day or two, before he could pick up the suitcase, a company employee happened upon the German uniforms and dutifully informed the president of the company. Dyby was sent for and told that if the "wrong" person had informed the Germans about the presence of the uniforms the whole factory building would have been blown up. Dyby says he shamefully replied that "we all have to take a few chances," but he realized the company president didn't want to see his factory flattened.

Because many of those involved in the transport work had been arrested or sent to Sweden for safety, by 1944 there was an extreme shortage of fishing skippers who still dared sail to Sweden and back, and there was competition among underground groups to utilize the remaining boats and their owners.

The Danish Navy's transport section, responsible for getting all military intelligence material to Sweden (and the Allies), had difficulty in finding reliable boat connections. Prom, a former language translator and teacher at the naval academy who went by the code name "Bertel," was chosen to represent navy intelligence transport to Sweden and the Allies. Prom and his co-workers tried to make a deal with Dyby's best skipper, Aage, but Dyby protested and demanded that they keep their hands off "his boats". He met with Prom and others a few times over Prom's favorite "sweet martinis" and discussed an arrangement whereby Dyby's "AA" boats and the DSRS would provide service at least twice a week for the intelligence service. (All fishing vessels had to be registered. The designation on the bow of boats from Copenhagen Nordhavn was AA and a number). Although there was some criticism from the Navy's transport office, the arrangement worked to their mutual satisfaction. In the remaining six months until the end of the war, "Dyby's AA boats" transported films, packages and weapons for the intelligence unit. At a meeting after the war, Prom declared that the military intelligence people were "ready to tear his head off" until he had found safe transport for their material.

Another member of Dyby's family was also working for the underground, although Knud found that out accidentally. While delivering messages and other material from Sweden to an underground group with ties to the large illegal newspaper *Frit Danmark* (Free Denmark), he visited a textile company in one of Copenhagen's back streets. To his surprise, one of the top leaders of the group was his cousin, Børge Olsen (Oløe). Says Dyby, "Once contact was established, he gave me mail to take to Sweden. I was able to bring material to him from contacts in Sweden, including news from the free world."

Many of the resistance workers themselves had to flee from Denmark because they were wanted by the Germans. If they had been caught, they could have been made to reveal information that would have jeopardized the work of their connections. Dyby was in constant danger and knew that he would have been sent to a concentration camp or executed if his work in the underground had been discovered. But despite the risks, he took pride in what he was doing--a free spirit helping wherever he was needed.

Dyby also gratefully remembers that many of his Danish friends in Sweden spent long nights and early mornings at sea in all kinds of weather, waiting to contact the boats from Denmark. Messages with information relating to longitude and latitude were not always clear and sometimes connections could not be made when there were German patrol boats to avoid, but stress and mishaps were all taken in stride as long as it meant a chance to "kick the Germans' behinds," says Dyby.

Toward the end of the occupation the resistance saboteurs were careful not to destroy too much of the machinery used in factories. As it became apparent that the Germans were losing the war, Danes realized they would again be the ones using the equipment when the war was over. To keep destruction to a minimum, Danes destroyed the power source to equipment, i.e., the transformers. It took the Germans a long time to repair the damage because the magnetic steel that was needed for the job was very scarce.

Getting downed Allied airmen to safety was one of the most adventuresome aspects of resistance work. Each story was different, but all reflected the courage and cooperation of the Danish people. One of the airmen helped by Dyby was twenty-three-year-old, American Charles Warren Dungan of Brownsville, Texas. In October 1944, Dungan's Mustang P-51 fighter plane was badly damaged when he participated in a raid on some factories in northern Germany. He was forced to bail out over Danish waters and paddled for hours in his small rubber raft until he got to the shore. Exhausted from his efforts, he was picked up by a fisherman and taken to a farm. There he was warmly received by the farmer's family, given hot food and an outfit of civilian clothes.

After resting for a day, Dungan was paired with a young man who had arrived at the farm on a tandem bike and the two pedaled to Copenhagen. In the city they went to one of the underground headquarters where the airman was teamed with another "helper."

Continuing the trip by bicycle, Dungan and his new guide met with Knud Dyby. While en route to their destination, Dyby and Charlie stopped in a restaurant and even though there were many German soldiers and sailors in the coffee shop all went well until Charlie took off his cap. He had the traditional American "crew cut." Dyby recalls, "I almost panicked because the crew cut was a sure giveaway. I got Charlie to put his cap back on fast. If the Germans had seen that American hairstyle, both Charlie and I would have been in serious trouble."

The pair went to North Harbor where Dyby put Dungan aboard a fishing boat. The airman was hidden behind the cabin siding, and a wood stove was placed in front of it so the Germans at the port would have a hard time detecting the hiding place. The fishing boat took off on its daily journey and soon met the DSRS's Swedish boat at the Swedish territorial water boundary. Hours later, Charles Dungan was on his way to Stockholm and from there back to England. In all this time no money had exchanged hands.

The DSRS files show that the group helped forty-four Allied airmen reach safety. The Danes were happy that in their own way they were able to help the Allies fight the hated enemy.

16

The Underground Press

Underground newspapers played an important role during the German occupation of Denmark. From the very beginning in April 1940, Danes realized they would not enjoy a free press. Over the course of the occupation some seven hundred different publications appeared, ranging from single sheets to editions with many pages. The regular daily newspapers were still being published, but since they were censored by the Germans, underground papers were considered a more reliable source of information. It was through these illegal papers that Danes were kept informed of what was really going on all over Europe, including the harassment and rounding up of Jews taking place in other occupied countries. Copies were passed from person to person and household to household.

One underground newspaper in particular, *Information*, became the prime source for accurate news. *Information* had been organized as a kind of underground Associated Press by a brilliant young journalist, Børge Outze. In early 1944, *Information* joined with Nordisk Nyhedstjeneste (Nordic News Service), and working together, 582 issues of *Information* were printed and distributed throughout the country. Stories focused on detailing the truth about sabotage, German counter-terrorism, Nazi imprisonment and murder, as well as news of the concentration camps and happenings in the free world.

Copies of the popular illegal underground publication were sent to the most important resistance groups and to the King. Every day at 10:00 a.m., Göthe Friberg, Swedish police commis-

Børge Outze, founder and editor of the "underground" Information News Agency. After escaping from German imprisonment, Knud Dyby arranged for his passage to Sweden.

sioner at Helsingborg, received the latest reports and newspapers, including *Information*, which he sent on to the Allied legations. Sometimes the material was microfilmed and inserted in a dummy spark plug in the engine of the plane that flew daily between Copenhagen and Malmö, Sweden. The resistance also saw to it that *every* boat going to Sweden was supplied with copies of *Information* to take along for distribution.

The mailing list of *Information* was a carefully guarded secret. If the Nazis had found the list, they would have had access to most of the resistance groups. In one case the Gestapo arrived at a house where the list was kept. They broke down the door, confronted the lady of the house and then searched the place, looking for signs of underground or illegal activity. Fortunately, the lady had seen the Germans coming and had hidden the list under an old blanket in her dog's basket. She sternly ordered her dog to "stay," and it obediently remained there while the house was searched. The Nazis did not find the list.

Because of his involvement with *Information*, Børge Outze quickly became one of the Gestapo's "most-wanted" Danes. On October 14, 1944, Outze, underground workers Dr. Mogens Fog and Arne Frem met with Knud Dyby to discuss the matter of some ammunition and explosives stored in a navy depot. At the end of the meeting Outze asked Dyby to join him at another meeting nearby, but Dyby had other plans at that time. An informer had told the Gestapo about the meeting Outze was to attend and the Germans barged in and arrested Outze, Dr. Fog, and a third underground worker, a restaurateur named Mikkelsen. A fourth person, Holbeck, tried to escape by going down the back stairs. He was shot and killed on the spot. Dyby remembers:

> *I did not expect to see Outze again after his arrest. But he was very bright and hoodwinked the Gestapo leaders by telling them he was as anti-Communist as they were. He promised to spy for them in Sweden and in December, 1944, they allowed him to "escape" when he was being taken from headquarters to prison. Dyby takes pride in the fact that when the Gestapo asked Outze if he wanted their*

help in getting him to Sweden, he told them, "No, I have better connections." The next day he secretly called Dyby and asked to be taken quickly to Sweden. Dyby immediately made the arrangements with one of his skipper contacts, and early in the morning Outze was hidden in a small fishing boat and on his way to safety.

Knud Dyby (light coat) and Baron Gustav Blixen-Finecke (dark coat) see Outze safely aboard a fishing boat on November 17, 1944. Outze had been arrested by the Gestapo on October 14 while attending a meeting at Gl. Kongevej 95. The picture was taken by Baron Blixen-Finecke's sister in an apartment overlooking the harbor.

17

A Danish
Concentration Camp

Tension mounted in the country when on August 28, 1943, the day before martial law was declared in Denmark, the first German execution of a Danish saboteur took place. In the months that followed, several hundred Danish citizens, Jews and non-Jews, were summarily deported without legal cause to concentration camps in Germany. The Danish Foreign Office protested the deportations, which were violations of international law, but the protests were ignored. In the fall of 1943 there was little concrete knowledge about the concentration camps, but there was general awareness and apprehension that conditions in the camps were very bad.

In January 1944, Niels Svenningsen, acting as head of the Foreign Office and speaking for the government, suggested the establishment of a camp specifically for internment of Danes arrested by the Germans. The building of the camp, to be located in Denmark, became a key factor in the negotiations that brought an end to the general strike in June of that year. After intense discussions the Germans agreed to allow the camp to be built with all expenses paid by the Danes. An understanding was reached that after the camp was opened, no more Danes would be deported and those who had been sent to other camps would be returned to Denmark. In the long run deportations did not stop, but many Danes were returned to Danish soil and saved from suffering and death in German concentration camps; this did not include Jews, who were not returned to the camp in Denmark.

Placed on the edge of Frøslev Plantation near the German-Denmark border in South Jutland, Frøslev Camp became a concentration camp like no other. Although there were watchtowers manned by guards night and day, and barbed-wire fences and land mines on the periphery, the camp itself was under Danish prison administration, a unique concession by the Nazis. Under this arrangement the Danes were in charge of prisoners' food and medical supplies, giving the Frøslev Camp an enormous advantage over other concentration camps.

The Germans wanted conditions to be as harsh as in other camps, but while life there was not pleasant it certainly was far superior to what was taking place elsewhere. Punishment was authorized for violation of rules, including uttering derogatory remarks about the guards, reporting sick without reason, refusing to work at forced labor, taking part in political discussions, holding divine services, spreading rumors, or helping or trying to help others to escape. In actuality, the guards were not particularly anxious to enforce the many rules and regulations and rarely did so. While Danish prisoners were often treated badly in German prisons by the Gestapo, this was rare in Frøslev Camp.

All prisoners except the elderly and sick were required to work. Divided into "parties," there was the mat-makers party, the roof-menders party, the waterworks party, the gravel pit party, etc., and each group made a concerted effort to maintain the appearance of work, but in truth all tried not to do anything that in any way might benefit the Germans.

Contact with the outside world was limited and sustained primarily through the use of illegal radio sets, with news passed from man to man. The Red Cross was able to help prisoners in many ways, including Christmas gifts and arranging for rare visits by relatives. The health of internees was much better in this camp than in others, as Danish doctors were among the prisoners. There was an infirmary and even a small operating room for minor surgeries. Vaccines were smuggled into the camp and all prisoners were inoculated against typhoid, cholera and dysentery, providing protection in case of transfer to a German concentration

A Danish policeman, Axel Munk-Andersen, made these drawings while imprisoned in Buchenwald Concentration Camp. (Reprinted from the book "September 19," published by Samlerens Forlag.)

camp where those diseases were prevalent.

The Germans had promised that once the camp was established there would be no more deportations of Danish citizens, but following the general strike of mid-September 1944, some 1700 members of the police force were arrested and sent from Copenhagen to Germany, primarily to the Neuengamme camp. This was followed almost immediately by the arrest of 300 more policemen from towns in Jutland and Funen, who first were sent to Frøslev Camp and then they, too, were deported to Germany.

Months later, in December, about 200 Danish prisoners were returned from Germany to Frøslev. They were policemen, all sick and elderly, and they were the first of a slow procession of returnees.

On April 22, 1945, Count Folke Bernadotte of Sweden visited Frøslev Camp. Count Bernadotte was related to the Swedish monarch and served as vice-president of the Swedish Red Cross. When he personally examined the conditions at the infirmary, a crowd of prisoners gathered outside and waited for him to appear. Then, very quietly, because such gatherings were strictly forbidden, they began to whistle and hum the Swedish national anthem, *Du gamla, du fria* (Thou Ancient, Thou Free), as their way of honoring him and his country. It was a moment no prisoner present that day would ever forget.

More than 12,000 prisoners passed through Frøslev Camp, that strange concentration camp where no one was tortured or murdered, where food and shelter and medical care were adequate, and where inmates knew there was a light at the end of the tunnel. The Danes had out-maneuvered the Germans one more time.

18

The White Bus Convoy

There were thousands of Danes and Norwegians, many of them policemen, who were prisoners in various concentration camps in Germany and elsewhere. In late 1944 and early 1945, representatives from Norway, Sweden and Denmark worked together on a plan to rescue as many of their countrymen as they could. Swedish Count Bernadotte was one of the organizers and leaders of the effort. The German chief of all concentration camp operations, Heinrich Himmler, who by this time was ready to distance himself from Hitler, was impressed by Bernadotte's connections and agreed to allow Scandinavians to be gathered in one place, in Neuengamme camp near Hamburg, Germany.

Then, in a masterful and miraculous stroke, Bernadotte also persuaded Himmler to allow the Scandinavians to be moved to Sweden. With the help of many others involved in the negotiations, especially Mr. H. H. Koch, Secretary of the Danish Ministry of Social Services, a fleet of Swedish and Danish buses was obtained. In the first week of April 1944, the Germans allowed a convoy to leave the camp; the convoy consisted of well over 100 white buses, six trucks and fifteen ambulances, plus smaller cars and motorcycles, along with ten doctors, sixteen nurses and hundreds of helpers. More than 10,000 prisoners from Neuengamme were transported across the German border through Denmark. Many of the buses were using "wood generators" as fuel, slowing them down, and some of the buses made the round trip more than once.

Thousands of Danes lined the road and cheered as the buses

Hundreds of Danish and Swedish Red Cross buses ready to depart for Germany in April 1945 to transport to Sweden thousands of prisoners held in German concentration camps.

made their way across the country en route to ferries which took them to Malmö, Sweden. Standing among the spectators on a sidewalk on the outskirts of Copenhagen was Knud Dyby, who looked on with tears in his eyes as he saw many of his old friends from the police force. "Although it was a day of relief and happiness for those of us who were watching, I could see that many of the former prisoners in the buses looked tired and ill, and I was also remembering the many police friends who had died in the camps."

Count Bernadotte, in his release negotiations with Himmler, had tried to include Danish Jews who were imprisoned in Theresienstadt, but even at that late date Himmler held firm to his Nazi principles and would not permit Jews to mix with other prisoners at Neuengamme. Bernadotte, who was concentrating on the convoy, turned the Theresienstadt problem over to Koch and Mrs. Hammerich, of the Danish Social Service Department, along with Hvass of the Foreign Ministry. Previously, Mrs. Hammerich, wife of Vice-Admiral Hammerich, and others had joined with the Red Cross to organize food and medical shipments to the Theresienstadt and Frøslev camps, as well as sending large shipments of these needed items to Norway, where they were in short supply. Now, Mrs. Hammerich, Mr. Koch and Mr. Hvass worked with Obersturmbannfuhrer Dr. Rennau, who was under direct orders from Himmler. Within two weeks, on April 15-16, 293 Danish Jews were released from Theresienstadt, transported through Jutland into Copenhagen, and from there by ferry to Malmö. Also in the "Bernadotte Actions" were some 10,200 women and children of various nationalities, mostly French and Polish, including women from Ravensbruck camp who had been rescued by the industrialist Oskar Schindler. (Their story has been told in the recent movie *Schindler's List*.) All were sent to Swedish camps in Tylösand and Strangnäs.

The role played by Count Bernadotte and his co-workers in rescuing so many prisoners from the clutches of the Nazis is a rare inspiring chapter to come out of the terrible period of the Holocaust.

Defeated Germans leaving Denmark in May 1945.

19

The End of the War

In the first three years of occupation, 1940-1943, the number of Danes involved in resistance activities could be counted only in the hundreds, but by the end of the war there were more than 35,000 freedom fighters working for a variety of groups. Within these groups friendships formed, carrying over into everyday lives to help and protect each other.

Those who were rescued often did not have a chance to thank their rescuers, partly because they hardly knew each other and partly because of the chaos at the time of rescue. False names, fake beards and dyed hair added to the confusion of identification. But Dyby remembers that two days after sending the first group on their way, he received a pound of prized real coffee beans from gentile friends who had hidden their Jewish neighbors, the Jacobsens. The accompanying card read, "Have been in Mynstedsvej (a district in Frederiksberg) and heard good news. And ask permission to say thanks." The card was signed by Ruth and Børge Møller Nielsen, friends of the Jacobsen family. Another note merely said, "In appreciation to one who owes 'Carlsen' many thanks for his rescue during the occupation." It was signed only "381 Madsen," the number of a saboteur Dyby helped escape and who then served as a member of the Danish Brigade in Sweden.

Dyby has a haunting memory of one occasion when he was thanked for his help. In March 1945, he and his police colleague, Frej, were invited to dinner with a family named Juul. Dyby and Frej had helped some of Juul's friends make their escape and the dinner was a happy celebration of appreciation. Two days later, acting on information supplied by the Danish resistance, the Royal

Air Force sent a fleet of bomber and fighter planes in a low altitude attack on Shell House, the Gestapo headquarters in the center of Copenhagen. The daring attack was successful but sadly, an unfortunate accident also sent bombs into the French school at nearby Frederiksberg and ninety-three children and many nuns were killed. Juul ran from his furrier shop and entered the burning school house. Thanks to his unselfish actions he saved some children -- but lost his life.

The Danes did not limit their help to getting the Jews to Sweden. In utterly unique circumstances, when the refugees returned to Denmark after the war, they found their homes and apartments, their factories and stores and their bank accounts had been protected. Damage that had been done during air raids was repaired and everything else was found exactly as it had been left. Women's groups had kept many of the homes and apartments clean, plants and gardens watered, and in some cases, a meal waiting for the owners on their return.

It is to the credit of the Danish nation that during the period when the Jews were gone from their country, there were few reports of vandalism to their property and, in the main, even criminals resisted the temptation to take advantage of the situation.

On the evening of May 4, 1945, the Germans surrendered in Holland, Norway and Denmark. The next morning, May 5, 1945, British troops were welcomed with kisses, flowers and flags as they crossed into Denmark. The Danish Brigade, whose members had been training in Sweden to fight the Germans should the land battle be carried to Denmark, crossed the Øresund and arrived in Helsingør. On this day, too, ships of the Danish navy and maritime fleet that had escaped the invasion were finally able to return to Danish ports.

Dyby remembers a humorous story from this joyous morning that could have resulted in tragedy:

> *Six o'clock on that historic morning found me with several Danish-Swedish Refugee Service men at Kastrup Harbor to meet a boat with over a dozen foreign newspaper reporters sent to cover Denmark during the Libera-*

110

tion. We were escorting the reporters to Copenhagen, but since we were ahead of the surrender time, I had to nego- tiate with a German soldier, asking him not to shoot at us just because we were a bit early. I clearly remember his relief in laying his gun aside and murmuring, "Gott sei dank!" (Thank God!) The war was over for him, and for all of us.

Denmark joyfully celebrated the end of the war and the end of the hated occupation. The king and the government returned to power. To mark the occasion, Dyby and some fellow resistance workers took a trip to Sweden to see the DSRS office before it was closed for good. In sharp contrast to earlier crossings, this one was not surrounded by secrecy and did not have to be made in the dead of night. There was no tension, no fear, no need to be unob- trusive, no hesitancy about the reception passengers would re- ceive upon their landing on Swedish soil. The former resistance workers joyfully crossed the Sound in a Chris Craft, a boat that had made the trip many times before. This time Dyby and his friends were able to use their own names and were happily wel- comed when they reached the harbor in Malmö, where for the first time they met many of the Swedish police, customs and navy personnel who had been helping the Danes for years.

Finally, returning to his job in the Frederiksberg Police Depart- ment, Dyby was told that all officers had to appear before the chief of police in his office and give a detailed account of their activities since the German raid on the department, September 19, 1944. They were required to report on whether they had been active in the underground, incarcerated in a concentration camp, had been a refugee in Sweden, or had gone into hiding without any other involvement during that period. "When it was my turn I told the chief that I had been involved in a lot of little things and, if he wished, he could look at that very day's publication of one of Copenhagen's largest newspapers in which there was my picture and a story about my resistance work and what I did to help trans- port refugees."

Dyby found that his police uniforms were missing from a hid-

Some of the boats owned by the Danish-Swedish Refugee Service on display at Copenhagen's "Langelinie" near the statue of "The Little Mermaid." These boats were later sold and the money given to help feed hungry, European children in the aftermath of World War II.

112

ing place in the attic of the building where he had been staying. "I hope the uniforms were 'organized' by freedom fighters and they made good use of them." Instead of being outfitted for new uniforms, however, Dyby looked upon the moment as an expedient time to make a career change and go back into the field of graphic arts.

The end of the war was a festive time. In the weeks that followed, Dyby was reunited with good friends who had been linked together in the underground. They celebrated with joyous parties and dinners, concerts and trips to the theater. The DSRS had some money left which could not be returned to the donors and Hendil, the DSRS chief, chose to mark the closing of the office with a celebratory "bang" by using the funds to organize a week called "Paris in Copenhagen". With strong support from Copenhagen's newspapers relating the activities of the DSRS, the highly successful week featured museum exhibits, French films and beautiful French models, auctions of champagne, and the sale of some of the fishing boats and speed boats used in the resistance. Dyby volunteered his services and supervised a streetcar that ran to the Royal Theater, with flags and fresh flowers decorating the cars, musicians and magicians on board and riders who were happy to donate 2 Kroner (32 cents) instead of the usual fee of 25 Øre (4 cents). Proceeds from the streetcar route and other events were donated to needy French children and to a Danish-Swedish committee giving help to children of deceased freedom fighters.

It was not long before the fishing fleet, those *Boats in the Night* that had been skippered by defiant, courageous, heroic fishermen, returned to its mundane task in the blue waters of the Sound. Peace had come at last.

Members of the Danish-Swedish Refugee Service celebrate the end of the war. Kneeling in the front row (left to right) are Kaj Sørensen (Ras), Knud Dyby (Carlsen), Jørgen Pollack, Henrik Kraft and Leif Hendil (Hot). Among the others are General Consul Julius Huttner, Baroness Elisabeth Blixen-Finecke and Countess Danneskiold-Samsøe.

20

After the War

For years after the end of the war, Danes did not talk about what they had done to rescue Danish Jews. There were two reasons for this: 1) Danish people, by their cultural tradition, are modest, and 2) because thousands of Danes helped in the rescue, the feeling was that "we all did something"--no one person needed to be singled out as special.

Only in recent years has the world begun to know and understand the real heroism that took place. Survivors as well as rescuers are now recalling their actions and the mixed emotions of that era--dismay at the time of the invasion, humiliation during the occupation, fear of the roundup, pride in the rescue and the feeling of unity in helping others.

What the Danes did was very impressive. Most of the 8,000 Danish Jews were rescued, sent to freedom and thus escaped the fate of their peers in other occupied countries. Thanks to vigilance and pressure, most of the remaining Danish Jews who nevertheless were in concentration camps survived. For those same reasons, most of the police who were sent to other camps also survived, as well as 11,000 Danes who were listed as enemies of the Nazis and were helped to Sweden. In the horror of the Holocaust, this is a unique record.

Dyby likes to quote a fellow resistance worker and rescuer, the late Otto Springer, who said, "The hand of compassion was sometimes faster than the calculus of reason." Dyby agrees and adds his own thoughts:

Surely, you felt as uneasy and apprehensive as the refu-
gees, but then you felt the compassion and strength, and
you knew that they were the ones who had to flee from
their previous comfortable existence, their homes and busi-
nesses, to go to a completely unknown future. You saw
their confidence in us, that we were able to help them.
Their words, their eyes and their nervous hands on your
arm blew away any hesitation you might have had. The
only thing that counted was to guide these unfortunate
people away from the Nazi madmen, away from arrest
and away from Germany's deadly concentration camps.

Knud Dyby still insists he was not special, that he only followed his conscience and was one of many whose deeds will forever
remain a testament to the inherent altruism and goodness of the
Danish people.

He who saves one life is as if he has saved the world.

The Talmud

Letter to Knud Dyby:

You represented that exceptional light and human brightness that helped shatter the darkness of the 'Kingdom of Night.' The story of rescue and resistance is the most important counterpoise in the perceptions of contemporary generations, for it speaks to the noblest to which humankind aspires -- and denies the passivity and culpability of the passive bystander.

Vladka Meed
Holocaust survivor, author, speaker

Knud Dyby points to his plaque on the commemorative wall in the Avenue of the Righteous of the Nations at Yad Vashem in Jerusalem.

118

Afterword

Following the Second World War, Knud Dyby immigrated to the United States where he worked in a variety of enterprises, including operating his own import-export company. In 1952, he was married to Elin Rasmussen, a young Danish woman who worked for the Danish Foreign Ministry. Two years later, they had a daughter Susanne who now holds a Ph.D. in biology and lives in Florida. In 1962, Dyby and his wife were divorced. Today, he is retired and lives in California.

In 1984 Dyby was invited to participate in a conference on the Holocaust held at the John F. Kennedy Center in Washington, D.C. The meeting was chaired by Elie Wiesel, a man who survived the concentration camps and who has spent his entire life working to assure that the horrors of the Holocaust are not forgotten. The experience provided the stimulus for Dyby to begin speaking about his wartime activities, especially his role in transporting Jewish Danes to safety in Sweden. In particular, he wants American school children to know what it means and how it feels to stand up for what is right, just because it is the right thing to do, regardless of personal danger or consequences.

Dyby's highest honor was an invitation to visit Yad Vashem, the memorial museum dedicated to the victims of the Holocaust located in Israel. At the time of his visit in April 1991, a bronze plaque engraved with the name *Knud Dyby* was placed on a commemorative wall in the Avenue of the Righteous of the Nations.

Knud Dyby is an old man now. He still stands straight and tall, and his eyes moisten when he recalls his resistance friends and police colleagues who died during the war.

He says, softly, "They are dead now. I speak to their memory."

Author's Acknowledgment

My guilt-laden knowledge of the Holocaust dates back to a conversation in Berkeley, California, in 1941. My mother said, "Look at this. *The Forward* (a daily, Jewish-American newspaper, printed in the Yiddish language) has these stories about something called concentration camps for Jews in Europe. It sounds terrible." In my vast superiority as an American born, university student, I replied to my immigrant mother, "Oh, Mama, if it isn't in the American newspapers, it can't be true." How wrong I was!

In 1974 one of my sons married the daughter of Rita and Isaac Haskell, survivors who endured many years of harsh treatment and deprivation in the concentration camps. The grandchildren of these survivors are my grandchildren too, and they have grown up with an intimate knowledge of the torture and death, the cruelty and pain that we now know as the Holocaust. Preserving this knowledge has become my concern.

In 1997 I received a letter from the Holocaust Oral History Project in San Francisco seeking writers who would put into written form some of the oral case histories they had videotaped. I responded with an offer of assistance and within days received a telephone call asking if I would like to write a book about Knud Dyby, a Danish-American who has been recognized for his role in helping rescue the Jews of Denmark in World War II.

I met with Mr. Dyby at his home in Novato, California, and was immediately charmed by his modest demeanor and convinced by his firm belief that the heroic efforts of his countrymen in World War II should be recorded in book form. He particularly wanted a memoir which would appeal not only to the general reading public but also to young adults as well.

Like many others, I was aware that Denmark had made a concerted effort to save its Jewish citizens from Hitler's concentration camps, but I knew few of the details. This book is the result of my unique learning experience about that period in history.

I would like to thank the Holocaust Oral History Project for suggesting this project and Knud Dyby for his invaluable assistance and consistent good humor in the time it has taken to complete the manuscript. Although Knud expressed concern his English was not as good as he thought it should be for such a project, he certainly conveyed to me, with distinct clarity, the emotions he still feels about the events related in this book.

My thanks to my colleagues, members of The Writers' Group in Modesto, California, who critiqued the manuscript-in-progress at our meetings and offered valuable and constructive suggestions. I am indebted to my friend and computer "guru," Elliott Ryder, for his patience in instructing me in the ways of computer technology, without which this book probably would not have been completed. I particularly appreciate the time and effort given by Professor Leo Goldberger of New York University for his review and comments regarding the text. I am grateful to my friend, Dr. Anne Gray, for research she contributed and her enthusiasm for this project. My special appreciation to my editor, Dr. John Mark Nielsen, for his expertise in reviewing numerous drafts of the manuscript and to his and Lur Publications unwavering commitment to telling Knud Dyby's story and the heroic actions of other Danes in the resistance. And finally, my thanks to my family and friends who repeatedly assured me that "even at my age"--79 at this writing--a first book was not an implausible idea. They did encourage me to hurry.

Martha Loeffler
1999

Bibliography

Block, Gay, and Malka Drucker. *Rescuers.* New York: Holmes & Meier, 1992.

Eisenberg, Azriel. *Witness to the Holocaust.* New York: Pilgrim Press, 1981.

Flender, Harold. *Rescue in Denmark.* New York: Holocaust Publications, 1963.

Friedlander, Albert H., ed. *Out of the Whirlwind: A Reader of Holocaust Literature.* New York: Schocken, 1976.

Gilbert, Martin. *The Holocaust: A History of the Jews of Europe During the Second World War.* New York: Holt, Rinehart, & Winston, 1986.

Goldberger, Leo, ed. *The Rescue of the Danish Jews: Moral Courage Under Stress.* New York: New York University Press, 1987.

Hæstrup, Jørgen. *Secret Alliance: A Study of the Danish Resistance Movement; 1940-1945.* Alison Borch-Johansen, Trans. 3 vols. Odense, Denmark: Odense University Press, 1976-1977.

Hilberg, Raul. *The Destruction of the European Jews.* New York: Holmes & Meier, 1983.

Kenneally, Thomas. *Schindler's List.* New York: Simon & Schuster, 1982.

Lampe, David. *The Danish Resistance.* New York: Ballantine Books, 1960.

Lowry, Lois. *Number the Stars.* New York: Dell Publishing, 1989. New York: Holmes & Meier, 1992.

Melchior, Marcus. *A Rabbi Remembers.* Werner Melchior, Trans. New York: Lyle Stuart, 1968.

Meltzer, Milton. *The Story of How Gentiles Saved Jews in the Holocaust.* New York: Harper & Rowe, 1968.

Meltzer, Milton. *Never to Forget: The Jews of the Holocaust.* New York: Dell, 1977.

Stræde, Therkel. *October 1943: The Rescue of the Danish Jews from Annihilation.* Copenhagen: Royal Danish Ministry of Foreign Affairs and the Museum of Danish Resistance 1940-1945, 1993.

Petrow, Richard. *The Bitter Years: The Invasion and Occupation of Denmark and Norway April 1940 - May 1945.* New York: William Morrow & Co., Inc., 1974.

Rabinowitz, Dorothy. *New Lives: Survivors of the Holocaust Living in America.* New York: Avon, 1976.

Rittner, Carol, and Sandra Myers, eds. *The Courage to Care.* New York: New York University Press, 1987.

Schoenberner, Gerhard. *The Yellow Star: The Persecution of the Jews in Europe, 1933-1945.* New York: Bantam, 1973.

Silver, Eric. *The Book of the Just: The Unsung Heroes Who Rescued Jews from Hitler.* New York: Grove Press, 1992.

Skov, Niels. *Letter to my Descendants.* Odense, Denmark: Odense University Press, 1997.

Sutherland, Christine. *Monica: Heroine of the Danish Resistance.* New York: Farrar Straus Giroux, 1990.

Thomas, John Oram. *The Giant-Killer: The Story of the Danish Resistance Movement, 1940-1945.* New York: Taplinger Publishing Co., 1976.

Werstein, Irving. *That Denmark Might Live: The Saga of the Danish Resistance in World War II.* Philadelphia: Macrae Smith Co., 1967.

Wiesel, Elie. *Night.* New York: Bantam, 1982.

Wiesel, Elie. *Memoir: All Rivers Run to the Sea.* New York: Schocken Books, 1995.

Yahil, Leni. *The Rescue of Danish Jewry: Test of a Democracy.* Morris Gradel, Trans. Philadelphia: Jewish Publication Society of America, 1969.

Additional background information, a file of photographs and the sources for data on page 76 are held in the Knud Dyby Collection (DYB 999) of the Danish Immigrant Archive - Dana College.

Index

Other books by Lur Publications

Tante Johanne
Letters of a Danish Immigrant Family
1887-1910
Letters and photographs with commentary by John W. Nielsen
118 pp. ISBN 0-930697-01-4
$12.95 plus shipping

Many Danes, Some Norwegians
Karen Miller's Diary - 1894
With photographs and commentary by John W. Nielsen
173 pp. ISBN 0-930697-02-2
$14.95 plus shipping

A Frame but no Picture
The story of a boy left behind in Denmark
Edited by John W. Nielsen
63 pp. ISBN 0-930697-03-0
$8.50 plus shipping

Embracing Two Worlds:
The Thorvald Muller Family of Kimballton
Edited by Barbara Lund-Jones & John W. Nielsen
180 pp. ISBN 0-930697-04-9
$14.95 plus shipping

Passages from India:
Letters, Essays, and Poems
1944-1946
by Norman C. Bansen
201 pp. ISBN 0-930697-05-7
$19.95 plus shipping

Order from: Lur Publications
Danish Immigrant Archive
Dana College
Blair, Nebraska 68008

 Lur Publications takes its name from the graceful bronze age horns found in Scandinavian museums. Just as today when those horns are blown, sounds from an ancient past are heard, so these books give voice to a less distant Danish American past.

Lur Publications Policies

Lur Publications is intended to encourage research and scholarship on Danish immigrant subjects as well as making available to the general public materials in the Danish Immigrant Archive - Dana College. As such Lur Publications complements the goals of the Danish American Heritage Society.

A further aim is to promote the collection, preservation, cataloging and use of written materials produced and received by Danish immigrants and their descendants. Such materials are welcomed by the respective Danish Immigrant Archives located at Dana College and Grand View College. Artifacts associated with Danish immigrants are sought by the Danish Immigrant Museum in Elk Horn, Iowa.

Scholars wishing to submit manuscripts for consideration are invited to contact Lur Publications, Danish Immigrant Archive, Dana College, Blair, Nebraska 68008-1041, (402) 426-7300, FAX: (402) 426-7332, e-mail: library@acad2.dana.edu

 # Lur Publications Personnel

General Editor: Dr. John W. Nielsen
Advisory Board: Dr. Myrvin Christopherson, Dr. Paul Formo, Dr. John Mark Nielsen, Ruth Rasmussen, Dorothy Willis
Library Staff: Dorothy Willis, Sharon Jensen, Mary Bacon, Marian Doicin, Thomas Nielsen
Student Assistants: Andrea Bjergaard, Kaj Nielsen, Leslie Schroeter
Archive volunteers (1998): Norman Bansen, John Chandler, Elaine Christensen, Ninna Engskow, Ann George, Edward Hansen, Florence M. Hansen, Shirley Hansen, Sara Hansen-Walter, Alice Hansen, Helga Hanson, Marilyn Hanson, Norlan Hanson, Verlan Hanson, Inga Hoifeldt, Ralf Hoifeldt, Jill Hennick, Michael Hennick, Ada Jeppesen, Herbert Jeppesen, Ruth Jeppesen, Dolores (Dody) Johnson, Oscar Johnson, Bernice (Bee) Krantz, Jeeraldine Kubicek, Inga Larsen, Lorraine Madsen, Margaret Madsen, Eunice Neve, Elizabeth Nielsen, John W. Nielsen, Luella Nielsen, Ruth Herman Nielsen, Dwayne Ohlsen, Lilliaan Ohlsen, Beverley Petersen, Dorothy Petersen, Richard Petersen, Ruth Rasmussen, Joan Sorensen, Dorte Staermose, Marion Sueordsen, Trine Thiessen, Marjorie Wahlgren, Dorothy Wright, Harold Wright.